Brian Heap
GCSE Series

LAW
Casebook
Second Edition

Edited by P A Read LLB, DPA, Barrister

HLT Publications

HLT PUBLICATIONS
200 Greyhound Road, London W14 9RY

First published 1991
Second edition 1993

© The HLT Group Ltd 1993

All HLT publications enjoy copyright protection and the copyright belongs to The HLT Group Ltd.

All rights reserved. No part of this publication may be reproduced or transmitted in any form or by any means, electronic, mechanical, photocopying, recording or otherwise, or stored in any retrieval system of any nature without either the written permission of the copyright holder, application for which should be made to The HLT Group Ltd, or a licence permitting restricted copying in the United Kingdom issued by the Copyright Licensing Agency.

Any person who infringes the above in relation to this publication may be liable to criminal prosecution and civil claims for damages.

ISBN 0 7510 0159 7

ACKNOWLEDGEMENT
The publishers and author would like to thank the Incorporated Council of Law Reporting for England and Wales for kind permission to reproduce extracts from the Weekley Law Reports.

British Library Cataloguing-in-Publication.

A CIP Catalogue record for this book is available from the British Library.

Printed and bound in Great Britain

CONTENTS

Foreword by Brian Heap		v
Preface		vii
Table of Cases		ix
1	General Principles	1
2	Criminal Law	11
3	Law of Tort	27
4	Contract and Consumer Law	39
5	Law Relating to Employment	83
6	Family Law	91

FOREWORD BY BRIAN HEAP

For those students who are interested in coming face to face with the fabric of society, GCSE Law is an admirable subject to study.

In addition to being introduced to basic rights and freedoms, the history of law, court structure and the work of solicitors, barristers and the judiciary, students will be introduced to criminal law, contracts, family law and law and the consumer.

Law at this level, however, is more than just another GCSE subject, it is an introduction to a possible career, many school and college leavers are aiming for a career in law by way of a university or college degree and it is not a decision to be taken lightly. A basic knowledge of the subject is an essential part of the decision-making process and both GCSE law and a course in 'A' level law will provide a preliminary insight into what will follow in a law degree and in a subsequent career in law.

You will find this book an excellent support for your GCSE studies including as it does the most up-to-date developments in law. Not only will it enable you to prepare the ground for success in the examination, it will also provide you with a sound foundation for 'A' level studies in both law and in the General Studies papers and an educational base for your future success.

Brian Heap

PREFACE

This HLT Casebook can be used as a companion volume to the *GCSE Law Textbook*; but it also comprises an excellent reference book in itself. Its aim is to supplement and enhance students' understanding of this particular area of the law. It is designed to be of particular use to those students who, studying at home, or for other reasons, do not have regular access to a law library. The book is divided into chapters and for ease of reference cases are arranged alphabetically within each chapter.

A brief word of explanation with regard to chapter arrangements follows. The Casebook, designed as it is as a companion volume to the Textbook, follows the same order. Most chapter heads are self-explanatory and cover the same ground as their counterparts in the Textbook: 'tort', 'contract', 'family law', and so on. Chapter 1, headed 'General Principles', gathers together all the preliminary material in the Textbook and covers the first general chapters. Inevitably, however, there is some overlap between different parts of the books and students will, where applicable, find cases cross-referred. For reasons of space, not every case mentioned in the Textbook could be included. Indeed, the brief reference accorded to some of the lesser cases in the Textbook is sufficient in itself. But more than 150 cases featuring in the Textbook have been reported in further detail in this Casebook.

Like the *GCSE Law Textbook*, this Casebook was first published in 1991. In this revised edition all recent developments in the law up to January 1993 have been taken into account.

TABLE OF CASES

Adams v Lindsell (1818) 1 B & Ald 681	39
Alaskan Trader, The (see Clea Shipping Corporation v Bulk Oil International Ltd)	
American Cyanamid Co v Ethicon Ltd [1975] AC 396; [1975] 2 WLR 316; [1975] 1 All ER 504	1, 39
Anglia Television Ltd v Reed [1972] 1 QB 60; [1971] 3 All ER 690	39
Ashbury Railway Carriage Co v Riche (1875) LR 7 HL 653	40
Attorney-General v Able [1984] QB 795; (1984) 78 Cr App R 197	11
Balfour v Balfour [1919] 2 KB 571	41
Beale v Taylor [1967] 1 WLR 1193	41
Beswick v Beswick [1968] AC 58; [1967] 3 WLR 932; [1967] 2 All ER 810	42
Blyth v Birmingham Waterworks Co (1856) 11 Exch 781	27
Bolton v Stone [1951] AC 850	27
Bridge v Campbell Discount Co Ltd [1962] AC 600; [1962] 2 WLR 439; [1962] 1 All ER 385	42
Brinkibon Ltd v Stahag Stahl und Stahlwarenhandelsgesellschaft mbH [1983] 2 AC 34; [1982] 2 WLR 264; [1982] 1 All ER 293	43
British Railways Board v Herrington [1972] AC 877; [1972] 2 WLR 537	28
Brogden v Metropolitan Railway Co (1877) 2 App Cas 666	43
Butler Machine Tool Co Ltd v Ex-Cell-O Corp (England) Ltd [1979] 1 WLR 401; [1979] 1 All ER 965	44
Byrne v Deane [1937] 1 KB 818	28
Byrne & Co v Leon van Tienhoven & Co (1880) 5 CPD 344	44
C v S [1987] 2 WLR 1108; [1987] 1 All ER 1230	11
Carlill v Carbolic Smoke Ball Co [1893] 1 QB 256	44
Casey's Patents, Re, Stewart v Casey [1892] 1 Ch 104	45
Central London Property Trust Ltd v High Trees House Ltd [1947] KB 130; [1956] 1 All ER 256	45
Christie v Davey [1893] 1 Ch 316	28
Clayton (Herbert) and Jack Waller Ltd v Oliver [1930] AC 209	83
Clea Shipping Corporation v Bulk Oil International Ltd, The Alaskan Trader [1984] 1 All ER 129	46
Clements v London and North Western Railway Co [1894] 2 QB 482	46
Collins v Godefroy (1831) 1 B & AD 950	46
Cook v Square D Ltd (1991) The Times 23 October	83
Cossey v UK [1991] 2 FLR 492; [1991] Fam Law 362	91
Costa v ENEL [1964] ECR 585	1
Cutter v Powell (1795) 6 Term Rep 320	47
D & C Builders Ltd v Rees [1966] 2 QB 617; [1966] 2 WLR 288; [1965] 3 All ER 837	47
D & F Estates Ltd v Church Commissioners for England [1988] 3 WLR 368; (1987) 7 Const LR 40	29
DPP v Camplin [1978] AC 705; [1978] 2 All ER 168	12
Dakin (H) & Co Ltd v Lee [1916] 1 KB 566	48
Daulia Ltd v Four Millbank Nominees Ltd [1978] Ch 231; [1978] 2 WLR 621 [1978] 2 All ER 557	49

TABLE OF CASES

Davis Contractors Ltd v Fareham Urban District Council [1956] AC 696; [1956] 2 All ER 145	49
De Francesco v Barnum (1890) 45 Ch D 430	50
Dickinson v Dodds (1876) 2 Ch D 463	50
Donoghue v Stevenson [1932] AC 562	29
Doyle v White City Stadium Ltd [1935] 1 KB 110	51
Dunlop Pneumatic Tyre Co Ltd v New Garage and Motor Co Ltd [1915] AC 79	51
Eastwood v Kenyon (1840) 11 Ad & El 438	51
Edwards v Skyways Ltd [1964] 1 WLR 349; [1964] 1 All ER 494	52
Entores Ltd v Miles Far East Corporation [1955] 2 QB 327; [1955] 3 WLR 48; [1955] 2 All ER 493	52
Eurymedon, The (see New Zealand Shipping Co Ltd v AM Satterthwaite & Co Ltd)	
Evans (J) & Son (Portsmouth) Ltd v Andrea Merzario Ltd [1976] 1 WLR 1078; [1976] 2 All ER 930	52
Fagan v Metropolitan Police Commissioner [1969] 1 QB 439; [1968] 3 All ER 442	13
Felthouse v Bindley (1862) 11 CB (NS) 869	53
Ffinch v Combe [1894] P 191	91
Fibrosa Spolka Akcyjna v Fairburn Lawson Combe Barbour Ltd [1943] AC 32; [1942] 2 All ER 122	53
Fisher v Bell [1961] 1 QB 394; [1960] 3 All ER 731	53
Flavell, Re, Murray v Flavell (1883) 25 Ch D 89	54
Foakes v Beer (1884) 9 App Cas 605	54
GCHQ Case, Council of Civil Service Unions v Minister for the Civil Service [1985] AC 374; [1984] 3 WLR 1174	2
Glasbrook Bros Ltd v Glamorgan County Council [1925] AC 270	55
Hadley v Baxendale (1854) 9 Exch 341	55
Harris v Nickerson (1873) LR 8 QB 286	56
Harvela Investments Ltd v Royal Trust Co of Canada (CI) Ltd [1986] AC 207; [1985] 3 WLR 276; [1985] 2 All ER 966	57
Heasmans v Clarity Cleaning Co Ltd [1987] IRLR 286; [1987] ICR 949	30
Hedley Byrne & Co Ltd v Heller & Partners [1964] AC 465; [1963] 2 All ER 575	30, 57
Herne Bay Steam Boat Co v Hutton [1903] 2 KB 683	57
Heron II, The (see Koufos v Czarnikow Ltd)	
Hill v Parsons (CA) & Co Ltd [1972] Ch 305; [1971] 3 WLR 995; [1971] 3 All ER 1345	58
Hivac Ltd v Park Royal Scientific Instruments Ltd [1946] Ch 169; [1946] 1 All ER 350	84
Holliday v National Telephone Co [1899] 2 QB 392	31
Holwell Securities Ltd v Hughes [1974] 1 WLR 155; [1974] 1 All ER 161	58
Honeywill & Stein Ltd v Larkin Bros (London's Commercial Photographers) Ltd [1934] 1 KB 191	31
Hudson v Ridge Manufacturing Co Ltd [1957] 2 WLR 948; [1957] 2 All ER 229	84
Hughes v Metropolitan Railway Co (1877) 2 App Cas 439	59
Hyde v Hyde (1866) 12 LT 235	92
Hyde v Wrench (1840) 3 Beav 334	59
Ibbetson, In the Goods of (1839) 2 Curt 337	92, 93
Jackson v Union Marine Insurance Co Ltd (1873) LR 10 CP 125	59
Jobson v Johnson [1989] 1 WLR 1026	60
Johnson v Agnew [1980] AC 367; [1979] 2 WLR 487; [1979] 1 All ER 883	2, 61
Jones, Re [1981] 2 WLR 106	93

Kennedy v Spratt [1972] AC 83	3
Kleinwort Benson Ltd v Malaysian Mining Corp Bhd [1989] 1 WLR 379; [1989] 1 All ER 785	61
Koufos v Czarnikow (C) Ltd, The Heron II [1969] 1 AC 350; [1967] 3 WLR 1491; [1967] 3 All ER 686	61
Krell v Henry [1903] 2 KB 740	62
Lawton v BOC Transhield Ltd [1987] 2 All ER 608	85
Leeds Industrial Co-operative Society v Slack [1924] AC 851	62
Lim Poh Choo v Camden and Islington Area Health Authority [1980] AC 174	3
Lister v Romford Ice and Cold Storage Co [1957] AC 555; [1957] 2 WLR 158; [1957] 1 All ER 125	3
Lumley v Wagner (1852) 1 De GM & G 604	63
McArdle, Re [1951] Ch 669; [1951] 1 All ER 905	63
Macarthys v Smith [1981] 1 All ER 111	4
McRae v Commonwealth Disposals Commission (1951) 84 CLR 377	63
McWilliams (or Cummings) v Sir William Arrol & Co Ltd [1962] 1 WLR 295	32
Maple Flock Co Ltd v Universal Furniture Products (Wembley) Ltd [1934] 1 KB 148	64
Mareva Compania Naviera SA v International Bulk Carriers SA, The Mareva [1980] 1 All ER 213	65
Maritime National Fish Ltd v Ocean Trawlers Ltd [1935] AC 524	65
Mersey Docks & Harbour Board v Coggins & Griffith (Liverpool) Ltd [1947] AC 1	32
Nash v Inman [1908] 2 KB 1	66
Nema, The (see Pioneer Shipping Ltd v BTP Tioxide Ltd)	
New Zealand Shipping Co Ltd v Satterthwaite (AM) & Co Ltd, The Eurymedon [1975] AC 154; [1974] 2 WLR 865; [1974] 1 All ER 1015	66
Page One Records Ltd v Britton [1968] 1 WLR 157; [1967] 3 All ER 822	67
Pao On v Lau Yiu Long [1980] AC 614; [1979] 3 WLR 435; [1979] 3 All ER 65	68
Paris v Stepney Borough Council [1951] AC 367	86
Parsons (H) (Livestock) Ltd v Uttley, Ingham & Co Ltd [1978] QB 791; [1977] 3 WLR 990; [1978] 1 All ER 525	68
Partridge v Crittenden [1968] 1 WLR 1204; [1968] 2 All ER 421	68
Payne v Cave (1789) 3 Term Rep 148	69
Payzu Ltd v Saunders [1919] 2 KB 581	69
Pepper (Inspector of Taxes) v Hart [1993] 1 All ER 42	4
Pharmaceutical Society of Great Britain v Boots Cash Chemists (Southern) Ltd [1953] 1 QB 401	70
Pinnel's Case (1602) 5 Co Rep 117a	70
Pioneer Shipping Ltd v BTP Tioxide Ltd, The Nema [1982] AC 724; [1981] 3 WLR 292; [1981] 2 All ER 1030	71
Planché v Colburn (1831) 8 Bing 14	71
Posner v Scott-Lewis [1986] 3 WLR 531	72
Price v Civil Service Commission [1978] IRLR 3	86
Protective Plastics v Hawkins (1964) 49 DLR 2d 496	87
R v Bingham [1991] Crim LR 43	14
R v Blaue [1975] 3 All ER 446; (1975) 61 Cr App R 271	14
R v Byrne [1960] 2 QB 396; [1960] 3 All ER 1	15
R v Cheshire (1991) 93 Cr App R 251	15
R v Church [1966] 1 QB 59	16
R v Clarke (1927) 40 CLR 227	72

TABLE OF CASES

R v Cunningham [1957] 2 QB 396	16
R v Dudley & Stephens (1884) 14 QBD 273	17
R v Dyson [1908] 2 KB 454; (1908) 1 Cr App R 13	18
R v Ghosh [1982] QB 1053; (1982) 75 Cr App R 154	18
R v Holden [1991] Crim LR 478	19
R v Jordan (1956) 40 Cr App R 152	19
R v Larsonneur (1933) 149 LT 542; (1933) 97 JP 206	20
R v Lawrence [1982] AC 510; [1981] 1 All ER 974	20
R v Morris; Anderton v Burnside [1983] 3 WLR 697	21
R v Secretary of State for Health, ex parte United States Tobacco International Inc [1991] 3 WLR 529	5
R v Seers [1985] Crim LR 315	22
R v Smith [1959] 2 QB 35; [1959] 2 All ER 193	22
R v Tolson (1889) 23 QBD 168	23
R v Williams; R v Davies (1991) The Times 23 October	23
Rashid v ILEA [1977] ICR 157	87
Ready Mixed Concrete (South East) Ltd v Minister of Pensions and National Insurance [1968] 2 QB 497; [1968] 2 WLR 775	33
Reardon Smith Line v Yngvar Hansen-Tangen [1976] 1 WLR 989; [1976] 3 All ER 570	72
Reid v Commissioner of Police of the Metropolis [1973] QB 551	73
Rondel v Worsley [1969] 1 AC 191; [1967] 3 WLR 1666; [1967] 3 All ER 993	5
Roscorla v Thomas (1842) 3 QB 234	73
Rose & Frank Co v Crompton (JR) Bros Ltd [1925] AC 445	74
Rothermere v Times Newspapers Ltdf [1973] 1 WLR 448	6
Routledge v Grant (1828) 4 Bing 653	74
Rowland v Divall [1923] 2 KB 500	74
Ryan v Mutual Tontine Westminster Chambers Association [1893] 1 Ch 116	75
Rylands v Fletcher (1868) LR 3 HL 330; (1866) LR 1 Ex 265	33
Saunders v Anglia Building Society [1970] 3 WLR 1078	75
Shanklin Pier v Detel Products Ltd [1951] 2 KB 854; [1951] 2 All ER 471	76
Shaw v DPP [1962] AC 220; [1961] 2 WLR 897; [1961] 2 All ER 446	6, 24
Sherras v De Rutzen [1895] 1 QB 918	24
Sim v Stretch [1936] 2 All ER 1237	7
Sinclair v Neighbour [1967] 2 WLR 1; [1966] 3 All ER 988	88
Sirros v Moore [1974] 3 WLR 459; [1974] 3 All ER 776	34
Smith v Leech Brain & Co Ltd [1962] 2 QB 405; [1962] 2 WLR 148	35
Stilk v Myrick (1809) 2 Camp 317; 6 Esp 129	77
Sturges v Bridgman (1879) 11 Ch D 852	35
Stokes v Anderson [1991] 1 FLR 391; [1991] Fam Law 310	93
Sweet v Parsley [1970] AC 132	7
Tarry v Ashton (1876) 1 QBD 314	35
Taylor v Caldwell (1863) 3 B & S 826	77
Thabo Meli v R [1954] 1 WLR 228; [1954] 1 All ER 373	25
Thomas v Thomas (1842) 11 LJ QB 104	77
Thorn v Meggitt Engineering Ltd [1976] IRLR 241	88
Tolley v J S Fry and Sons Ltd [1931] AC 333	36
Twine v Bean's Express Ltd [1946] 1 All ER 202; (1946) 62 TLR 458; (1946) 175 LT 131	36
Universe Tankships Inc of Monrovia v International Transport Workers' Federation [1982] 2 WLR 803	37, 78

Van Duyn *v* Home Office [1974] ECR 1337; [1974] 1 WLR 1107	7
Van Gend en Loos Case [1963] ECR 1	8
Varley *v* Whipp [1900] 1 QB 513	78
Victoria Laundry (Windsor) Ltd *v* Newman Industries Ltd [1949] 2 KB 528; [1949] 1 All ER 997	79
Ward *v* James [1966] 1 QB 273	8
Warner Bros Pictures Inc *v* Nelson [1937] 1 KB 209; [1936] 3 All ER 160	79
Wheat *v* E Lacon & Co Ltd [1966] AC 522; [1966] 2 WLR 581	37
Wilkinson *v* Downton [1897] 2 QB 57	38
Williams *v* Roffey Bros & Nicholls (Contractors) Ltd [1990] 1 All ER 512	80
Woodhouse *v* Brotherhood [1972] 3 WLR 215; [1972] 3 All ER 91	89
Woodhouse AC Israel Cocoa Ltd SA *v* Nigerian Produce Marketing Co Ltd [1972] AC 741; [1972] 2 WLR 1090; [1972] 2 All ER 271	80
Wroth *v* Tyler [1974] Ch 30; [1973] 2 WLR 405; [1973] 1 All ER 897	81

1 GENERAL PRINCIPLES

American Cyanamid Co v Ethicon Ltd [1975] AC 396 House of Lords (Viscount Dilhorne, Lords Diplock, Cross, Salmon and Edmund-Davies)

Interlocutory injunctions

Facts

The plaintiff owned a patent relating to design and manufacture of surgical stitches. The defendants were about to market a product which, it was claimed, infringed that patent. The plaintiffs applied for an interlocutory injunction to restrain the launch pending trial of the action.

Held

The injunction should be granted. Leaving aside the complicated scientific evidence which supported and denied the claim, the balance of convenience favoured restraint upon a venture which had not yet been put into effect. Lord Diplock stated:

> 'My Lords, when an application for an interlocutory injunction to restrain a defendant from doing acts alleged to be in violation of the plaintiffs' legal right is made on contested facts, the decision whether or not to grant an interlocutory injunction has to be taken at a time when ex hypothesi the existence of the right or the violation of it, or both, is uncertain and will remain uncertain until final judgment is given in the action ... The object of the interlocutory injunction is to protect the plaintiff against injury by violation of his right for which he could not adequately be compensated in damages recoverable in the action if the uncertainty were resolved in his favour at trial; but the plaintiff's need for such protection must be weighed against the corresponding need of the defendant to be protected against injury resulting from his having been prevented from exercising his own legal rights for which he could not be adequately compensated under the plaintiff's undertaking in damages if the uncertainty were resolved in the defendant's favour.'

See also Chapter 4.

Costa v ENEL 6/64 [1964] ECR 585 Court of Justice of the European Communities

European Community legislation

Facts

A lawyer in Milan refused to pay an electricity bill, arguing that the recent nationalisation of the Italian electricity industry was contrary to several articles in the EEC treaty. The Milanese judge referred the case to the ECJ for interpretation under article 177.

Held

The court had jurisdiction under article 177 to hear the case. It considered article 37(2) which creates individual rights to protect community nationals and prohibits any new rule which discriminates between nationals of member states in regard to monopolies. Since the nationalisation constituted subsequent domestic legislation which conflicted with the treaty, it was not enforceable.

Maurice Lagrange M:

> 'The common market system is based on the creation of a legal order separate from that of the member states, and if we reached the stage where a constitutional judge of one of the member states feels that ordinary national laws which are contrary to the treaty could prevail over the treaty without any judge having the power to nullify their application so that they could only be repealed or

modified by parliament, such a decision would create an insoluble conflict between the two orders and would undermine the very foundations of the treaty.'

GCHQ Case, Council of Civil Service Unions v Minister for the Civil Service
[1985] AC 374 House of Lords (Lords Fraser, Scarman, Roskill, Dillon and Brightman)

Judicial review of the royal prerogative.

Facts

Acting pursuant to delegated prerogative power, Article 4 of the Civil Service Order in Council 1982, the Minister for the Civil Service (the Prime Minister) issued an oral instruction to the unions representing those civil servants employed at Government Communications Headquarters (GCHQ), altering the conditions of service so as to prohibit membership of trade unions by the civil servants employed there. Past practice had been for the Prime Minister to consult the unions at GCHQ before making such changes. The reason for not doing so on this occasion was a fear that the proposed changes might prompt industrial action at GCHQ, which would have a deleterious effect on national security.

Two questions fell to be considered by the House of Lords. Firstly, whether the exercise of prerogative power by the Prime Minister was reviewable, and secondly, if it was, whether the use of such power had been contrary to the rules of natural justice due to lack of prior consultation.

On the reviewability of prerogative power:

Held

Delegated prerogative power was not immune from judicial review; the scope of such powers could be ascertained by reference to their object, or procedure by which they were to be exercised. The justiciability of the matter in dispute was a more relevant factor than the source of the power being exercised. The declaration sought by the union was refused on other grounds however.

Johnson v Agnew [1980] AC 367 House of Lords (Lords Wilberforce, Salmon, Fraser, Keith and Scarman)

Overruling and reversing

Facts

The plaintiff owned property which had been mortgaged to the defendants, but was in arrears with his repayments. He agreed to sell the property to a purchaser for a sum well in excess of the mortgage but, when the purchaser failed to complete, obtained an order for specific performance. Nine months later, the order for specific performance not having been carried out, the defendant mortgagees enforced their security by selling the property. The proceeds realised by the mortgage were insufficient to discharge the mortgage in full, and the plaintiff applied for an order that the purchaser should pay the balance of the purchase price to him.

Held

Although a vendor had to elect at the trial whether to pursue the remedy of specific performance or that of damages, if specific performance was ordered the contract remained in effect and was not merged in the judgment so that, if the order was not complied with, he might apply to the court to put an end to the contract and, if he did so, he was entitled to damages appropriate to the breach of contract.

Lord Wilberforce:

> 'In my opinion *Henty* v *Schroder* (1879) 12 Ch D 666 cannot stand against the powerful tide of logical objection and judicial reasoning. It should no longer be regarded as of authority: the cases following it should be overruled. In particular *Barber* v *Wolfe* and *Horsler* v *Zorro* cannot stand so far as they are based on the theory of "rescission ab initio" which has no application to the termination of a contract on accepted repudiation.'

See also Chapter 4.

Kennedy v Spratt [1972] AC 83 House of Lords (Lord Reid, Lord Morris of Borth-y-Gest, Lord Wilberforce and Lord Diplock)

House of Lords - votes equally divided

Facts

In the context of two Northern Ireland statutes, a question arose as to the meaning of the expression 'sentenced to imprisonment'. Lord Upjohn had also been present throughout the hearing, but he died before the speeches were delivered.

Held (Lord Morris of Borth-y-Gest and Lord Wilberforce dissenting)

The words in question meant 'sent to prison' and, as the votes were equal, in accordance with standing orders and the ancient rule semper praesumiter pro negarite, the appeal would be dismissed.

Lim Poh Choo v Camden & Islington Area Health Authority [1980] AC 174 House of Lords (Viscount Dilhorne, Lords Diplock, Simon of Glaisdale and Scarman)

Damages - law reform

Facts

Having been admitted to hospital for a minor operation, the plaintiff suffered irreparable brain damage, due to the defendants' negligence. Damages were awarded for pain, suffering and loss of amenities, loss of earnings, cost of future care and future inflation. Both parties appealed.

Held

Both appeals would be dismissed.

Lord Scarman:

> 'It cannot be said that any of the time judicially spent on these protracted proceedings has been unnecessary. The question, therefore, arises whether the state of the law which gives rise to such complexities is sound. Lord Denning MR in the Court of Appeal declared that a radical reappraisal of the law is needed. I agree. But I part company with him on ways and means. Lord Denning MR believes it can be done by the judges, whereas I would suggest to your Lordships that such a reappraisal calls for social, financial, economic and administrative decisions which only the legislature can take. The perplexities of the present case, following on the publication of the report of the Royal Commission on Civil Liability and Compensation for Personal Injury ("the Pearson report"), emphasise the need for reform of the law.
>
> The course of the litigation illustrates, with devastating clarity, the insuperable problems implicit in a system of compensation for personal injuries which (unless the parties agree otherwise) can yield only a lump sum assessed by the court at the time of judgment. Sooner or later, and too often later rather than sooner, if the parties do not settle, a court (once liability is admitted or proved) has to make an award of damages. The award, which covers past, present and future injury and loss, must, under our law, be of a lump sum assessed at the conclusion of the legal process. The award is final; it is not susceptible to review as the future unfolds, substituting fact for estimate. Knowledge of the future being denied to mankind, so much of the award as is to be attributed to future loss and suffering (in many cases the major part of the award) will almost surely be wrong. There is really only one certainty; the future will prove the award to be either too high or too low.'

Lister v Romford Ice and Cold Storage Co Ltd [1957] AC 555; [1957] 2 WLR 158 House of Lords (Lords Simonds, Morton, Radcliffe, Tucker and Somervell)

Breach of contractual duty of care

Facts

A lorry driver, employed by the company, took his father with him as mate. In backing the lorry negligently he injured his father who, subsequently, recovered damages from the company for his son's negligence. The company sued the son claiming that he had broken an implied term in his contract to exercise reasonable skill and care in driving.

Held

The appeal would be dismissed; the driver was under a contractual obligation of care to his employers in performance of his duties; the company could recover damages from him.

Simonds LJ stated that it was trite law that a single act of negligence might give rise to a claim either in tort or for breach of an implied term, express or implied, in a contract. Of this the negligence of a servant in performance of his duty was a clear example.

The appellant was under a contractual obligation of care in performance of his duty; he committed a breach of it, the respondents thereby suffered damage and they were entitled to recover that damage from him.

Macarthys Ltd v Smith [1981] 1 All ER 111 Court of Justice of the European Communities. Court of Appeal (Lord Denning MR, Lawton and Cumming-Bruce LJJ)

Community law

Facts

The applicant was employed to manage a stock room at a wage of £50 a week. She claimed that, under the Equal Pay Act 1970, she was entitled to £60 a week, the wage paid to her male predecessor.

Held

On appeal, the Court of Appeal held that the 1970 Act did not prevent an employer from paying a female employee less than a male for the same job, but referred the case to the Court of Justice of the European Communities which (applying article 119) held that, since she was doing equal work to the man, even though not contemporaneously, she had a right to equal pay. The Court of Appeal therefore dismissed the employers' appeal.

Since the European Communities Act 1972 had made EEC law part of the United Kingdom law, and since the EEC has priority over conflicting domestic law, both systems should be considered by the court.

Pepper (Inspector of Taxes) v Hart [1993] 1 All ER 42 House of Lords (Lord Mackay of Clashfern, Lords Keith, Bridge, Griffiths, Ackner, Oliver and Browne-Wilkinson)

Statutory interpretation

Facts

In assessing tax payable by Mr Hart and nine others, who at the relevant time were members of the staff of Malvern College, the tax inspector assessed the value of a concessionary fees system at the college for children of the staff as being the normal cost of fees. The staff obtained these concessionary rates because of the fact that they were 'low band' taxpayers. To assess tax payable on the basis that they were receiving benefits from their employer valued on the normal fee system would raise the amount of tax payable and they would no longer qualify for concessionary fees.

Held

Value of the concessionary rates should be quantified on the basis of the marginal costs to the employer. In construing the provisions of s63 of the Finance Act 1976 too literally, it would in this case lead to absurdity. The House of Lords held that as an aid to construing statutes which if construed too literally would be ambiguous or obscure, *Hansard* might be consulted for reports of speeches or debates. Such assistance might only be sought if the items reported in *Hansard* would give a court some idea of exactly what the Act was aimed at achieving or what mischief it sought to prevent.

R v Secretary of State for Health, ex parte United States Tobacco International Inc [1991] 3 WLR 529 Queen's Bench Division, Divisional Court (Taylor LJ and Morland J)

Validity of delegated legislation - proportionality of measure - fairness in introduction

Facts

The applicants owned a company that produced an oral snuff product, sold under the trade name 'Skoal Bandits'. The Department of Trade and Industry and the Scottish Office had encouraged the applicants to set up a factory for the manufacture of the product in Scotland and had made available incentives in the form of government grants. The applicants' factory opened in East Kilbride in 1985. Earlier, in 1977, the Committee on Carcinogenicity of Chemicals in Food, Consumer Products and the Environment (COC) was established to advise the government. On the advice of COC the government negotiated an agreement with the applicants whereby they would not sell their product to persons under the age of 18, and would include a health warning on the packaging. In June 1986, the COC revised its view of oral snuff and advised the government that the product should be banned. In February 1988, the Secretary of State for Health announced his intention to introduce regulations banning the sale of oral snuff products in the United Kingdom, exercising his powers under the Consumer Protection Act 1987. Section 11(5)(a) of the 1987 Act required the Secretary of State to consult those substantially affected by the proposed ban. The applicants sought details of the evidence relied upon by the government, but there was considerable delay on the part of the Secretary of State in responding, and even then the Secretary of State had refused to reveal all the evidence that the government had received. The applicants were not informed of the gist of the COC's views until October 1988, and were refused access to the full report. The regulations came into effect on 13 March 1990.

The applicants sought judicial review of the decision of the Secretary of State to make the regulations on the grounds (inter alia) that the regulations were a disproportionate response to the health danger posed by oral snuff, and that the Secretary of State had acted unfairly in not consulting fully before making the regulations. The applicants relied also on the fact that they had been encouraged to develop sales of the product in the United Kingdom by the government.

Held

The application would be allowed, and an order of certiorari granted to quash the regulations. It was held, inter alia, that the manufacturers had no legitimate expectation that there would be no ban but that in view of the history of their relationship with government the statutory consultation period was inadequate and that further the company should have had a full opportunity to know and respond to the evidence on which the government had relied.

Rondel v Worsley [1967] 3 WLR 166 House of Lords (Lords Reid, Morris, Pearce, Upjohn and Pearson)

Facts

W was a barrister and had on a dock brief represented R who had been convicted and sent to prison. R then brought an action against W for professional negligence. The case reached the House of Lords on the legal point of whether such an action could lie. The question of negligence never came before the court.

Held

An action did not lie against W for negligence. Obiter, it was observed that a barrister cannot be sued for negligence for the conduct of his case in court. This is not due to the absence of any contract but is a rule based on public policy.

Rothermere v Times Newspapers Ltd [1973] 1 WLR 448 Court of Appeal (Lord Denning MR, Cairns and Lawton LJJ)

The jury in civil cases

Facts

On 19 March 1971 *The Times* newspaper published an article entitled 'Profit and Dishonour in Fleet Street' by Mr Bernard Levin.

It concerned the closing of one newspaper and the continuance of another by the newspaper group. The plaintiffs, a former chairman, the present chairman and the group brought a libel action against the defendants, the editor, the publishers and the author, claiming that the article alleged that the group was badly run and had brutally shut down a newspaper for bogus reasons of economy, when the true reason was to increase their profits, causing great hardship to their faithful staff.

The defendants raised the defences of justification and fair comment on a matter of public interest and the plaintiffs alleged malice. A great number of documents were to be examined in evidence. The particulars of defence ran to 59 pages and the plaintiffs' list of documents contained 2,033 items, many of which were files.

The defendants requested trial by jury under s6(1) Administration of Justice (Miscellaneous Provisions) Act 1933. The plaintiffs appealed contending that the case fell within the exception 'the trial thereof requires prolonged examination of documents or accounts which cannot conveniently be tried with a jury'. Trial by judge alone was ordered. The defendants appealed.

Held (Cairns LJ dissenting)

The appeal would be allowed. Although the trial would require 'prolonged examination' of documents within the meaning of the Act issues of material importance had been raised and weight should be attached to them. The judge had failed to consider this in the exercise of his discretion and trial by jury should be ordered. (Per Cairns LJ: a fair result would be more likely to be achieved by trial with a judge alone.)

Order reversed.

Shaw v DPP [1962] AC 220 House of Lords (Viscount Simonds, Lords Reid, Tucker, Morris and Hodson)

Judicial law making

Facts

A conspiracy to corrupt public morals was an offence. The defendant had agreed to publish a 'Ladies Directory' containing names, addresses, photographs and other details of prostitutes.

Held

He had been rightly convicted of conspiracy to corrupt public morals.

Viscount Simonds:

'In the sphere of criminal law, I entertain no doubt that there remains in the courts of law a residual power to enforce the supreme and fundamental purpose of the law, to conserve not only the safety and the order but also the moral welfare of the state, and that it is their duty to guard it against attacks which may be the more insidious because they are novel and unprepared for.'

See also Chapter 2.

Sim v Stretch [1936] 2 All ER 1237 House of Lords (Lords Atkin, Russell and Macmillan)

The jury

Facts

The plaintiff's housemaid went to work for the defendant. The defendant sent a telegram to the plaintiff containing the following message: 'Edith has resumed her service with us today. Please send her possessions and the money you borrowed, also her wages to Old Barton - Sim'. The plaintiff claimed damages for libel, alleging that these words were defamatory, implying that the plaintiff was in financial difficulties, had been forced to borrow money from his housemaid, had been unable to pay her wages and was uncreditworthy.

Held

There had been no libel since the words were not reasonably capable of a defamatory meaning.

Sweet v Parsley [1970] AC 132 House of Lords (Lords Reid, Morris, Pearce, Wilberforce and Diplock)

Presumptions

Facts

The appellant was the sub-tenant of a farmhouse and let out rooms to tenants. She no longer lived there herself but retained a room and returned occasionally to collect rent and mail. Drugs were found on the property and she was charged with being 'concerned in the management' of premises used for drug taking subject to s5 of the Dangerous Drugs Act 1965. The prosecutor conceded that she was unaware of the existence of the drugs. She was convicted of the offence.

Held

Lord Diplock approved *R v Tolson* (1889) 23 QBD 168 in his judgment, saying that it laid down:

'... as a general principle of construction of any enactment, which creates a criminal offence, that, even where the words used to describe the prohibited conduct would not in any other context connote the necessity for any particular mental element, they are nevertheless to be read subject to the implication that a necessary element in the offence is the absence of a belief, held honestly and upon reasonable grounds, in the existence of the facts, which, if true, would make the act innocent.'

Van Duyn v Home Office [1974] 1 WLR 1107 High Court (Pennycuick V-C)

Community law

Facts

The plaintiff, a Dutch national, sought to enter the United Kingdom to work at a Scientology establishment in Sussex. The Home Office regarded the entry of foreign nationals to work or study at the establishment as being contrary to public policy and she was refused leave to enter. She brought an action against the Home Office for a declaration that she was entitled under article 48 of the EEC treaty to enter and work in the United Kingdom.

The plaintiff applied to the High Court for a reference to the European Court for a preliminary ruling under article 177 on the questions of whether the refusal of entry was based on personal conduct or whether article 48 of the treaty conferred on her a right of entry enforceable in United Kingdom courts. The Home Office argued that article 48 did not confer a right of entry which she could enforce in the United Kingdom courts, and that the refusal of entry was based on her previous personal conduct as a Scientologist.

Held

The point should be referred to the European Court for interpretation of the issue of whether the refusal of entry was based exclusively on the plaintiff's personal conduct.

Van Gend en Loos v Netherlands Fiscal Administration Case 26/62 [1963] ECR 1

Community law

Facts

The plaintiff objected to paying an import duty of 8 per cent when the tariff under article 12 was only 3 per cent. The question considered by the European Court concerned whether an article of the EEC treaty conferred rights on individual citizens of the EEC which a national judge must enforce.

Held

The community constitutes in international law a new rule of law in favour of which the states have, in a limited measure, restricted their sovereignty and under which not only the member states but their subjects too have rights. In the same way as community law creates, independently of legislation of the member states, obligations for private parties, it is also able to create rights which private parties can make applicable on their own behalf.

Ward v James [1966] 1 QB 273 Court of Appeal (Lord Denning MR, Sellers, Pearson, Davies and Diplock LJJ)

Civil juries

Facts

The plaintiff was serving in the British Army in West Germany. On 20 May 1962 he was travelling as a passenger in the defendant's car and as the result of an accident he sustained severe injuries leaving him a permanent quadriplegic. On 14 December 1962 an action was brought on behalf of the plaintiff against the defendant for damages for negligence. The substantial question was the amount of damages to be awarded. On 23 July 1963 the Master ordered trial by jury at the request of the plaintiff.

On 30 July 1963 the defendant appealed to the judge but this was dismissed. Between the following March and July the parties were negotiating a settlement and the case was finally set down for trial in July 1984. On 26 October 1964 the defendant's application for leave to appeal against the order for trial by jury was dismissed and in November 1964 he appealed to the Court of Appeal for leave to appeal out of time and also requested that the trial should be without a jury.

Held

1) Leave to appeal out of time would be granted, the principles applicable to final appeals not being equally applicable to interlocutory appeal especially where the mode of trial is in question. The fact that the action was some way from the trial stage and that the position regarding the appropriateness of jury trials was in question in cases of personal injuries was also taken into account.

2) The court could review the exercise of the judge's discretion concerning the mode of trial, however, it would not do so in these circumstances as the defendant had acquiesced for too long in the trial judge's order and the court also had regard to the fact that in the future the Court of Appeal would be less hesitant in upsetting a jury's award where it was seriously wrong.

Appeal dismissed.

2 CRIMINAL LAW

Attorney-General v Able [1984] QB 795 Queen's Bench Division (Woolf J)

Use of the civil courts to determine a criminal matter

Facts

The respondent was a member of the executive committee of the organisation 'EXIT', which promoted euthanasia. The society had published a booklet entitled 'A guide to self deliverance', which gave advice on how those who wished to commit suicide might successfully do so. The Attorney-General adopted the view that the publication might constitute an offence under s2(1) of the Suicide Act 1961, but instead of instigating a criminal prosecution against members of the society's executive committee, he sought a declaration in the High Court that the publication would be a violation of the criminal law. The respondents argued that this was an inappropriate procedure where a point of criminal law was in question.

Held

The civil courts should exercise great restraint in granting declarations on points of criminal law, so as to avoid usurping the function of the criminal courts. Where there was evidence that the booklet in question was supplied to a person who was known to be contemplating suicide, with the intention that this should encourage the commission of the suicide, and that suicide did result, the supply of the booklet could amount to an offence of aiding and abetting suicide. In the present case there was no evidence to suggest that the booklet was to be supplied with such an aim in mind, the declaration would therefore be refused.

C v S [1987] 2 WLR 1108 Court of Appeal (Civil Division) (Sir John Donaldson MR, Stephen Brown and Russell LJJ)

Whether abortion at 18-21 weeks of gestation is an offence under the Infant Life (Preservation) Act 1929

Facts

The plaintiff sought an injunction to prevent the defendant, who was pregnant with his child, from going ahead with an abortion. He claimed (inter alia) that as the foetus had reached between 18 and 21 weeks of gestation, it was a 'child capable of being born alive' within the meaning of the Infant Life (Preservation) Act 1929. His claim rested on the assertion that an injunction should be granted either to himself, as the prospective father, or to the unborn child, to prevent the commission of what would be an offence under the 1929 Act.

Held at first instance

The application would be refused.

Held on appeal to the Court of Appeal

The appeal would be dismissed.

Sir John Donaldson MR:

> 'We have no evidence of the state of the foetus being carried by the first defendant, but if it has reached the normal stage of development and so is incapable ever of breathing, it is not in our judgment "a child capable of being born alive" within the meaning of the Act and accordingly the termination of this pregnancy would not constitute an offence under the Infant Life (Preservation) Act 1929.'

DPP v Camplin [1978] AC 705 House of Lords (Lords Diplock, Morris, Simon, Fraser and Scarman)

Reasonable man test for provocation

Facts

The defendant was a 15-year-old boy who, having been buggered by the deceased, was then taunted by him. The defendant killed the deceased by hitting him over the head with a chapatti pan. He was convicted of murder following a direction by the trial judge to the jury that they were to judge the defendant by the standard of the reasonable adult, not a reasonable 15 year old boy. The Court of Appeal allowed the appeal on the basis that the more subjective test, which took account of the defendant's age, should have been applied. The Crown appealed to the House of Lords.

Held

The appeal would be dismissed. Because of the importance of this case and the fact that it impinges on other cases, it is worth quoting, at some length, extracts from the judgment of Lord Diplock:

'In his address to the jury on the defence of provocation ... counsel for Camplin, had suggested to them that when they addressed their minds to the question whether the provocation relied on was enough to make a reasonable man do as Camplin had done, what they ought to consider was not the reaction of a reasonable adult but the reaction of a reasonable boy of Camplin's age. The judge thought that this was wrong in law. So in his summing-up he took pains to instruct the jury that they must consider whether -

"... the provocation was sufficient to make a reasonable man in like circumstances act as the defendant did. Not a reasonable boy, as ... (counsel for Camplin) would have it, or a reasonable lad; it is an objective test - a reasonable man."

The jury found Camplin guilty of murder. On appeal the Court of Appeal (Criminal Division) allowed the appeal and substituted a conviction for manslaughter on the ground that the passage I have cited from the summing-up was a misdirection. The court held that -

"... the proper direction to the jury is to invite the jury to consider whether the provocation was enough to have made a reasonable person of the same age as the appellant in the same circumstances do as he did."

The point of law of general public importance involved in the case has been certified as being:

"Whether, on the prosecution for murder of a boy of 15, where the issue of provocation arises, the jury should be directed to consider the question, under section 3 of the Homicide Act 1957 where the provocation was enough to make a reasonable man do as he did by reference to a 'reasonable adult' or by reference to a 'reasonable boy of 15' ..."

... [U]ntil the 1957 Act was passed there was a condition precedent which had to be satisfied before any question of applying this dual test could arise. The conduct of the deceased had to be of such a kind as was capable in law of constituting provocation; and whether it was or not was a question for the judge, not for the jury. The House so held in *Mancini* v *DPP* [1942] AC 1 where it also laid down a rule of law that the mode of resentment, as for instance the weapon used in the act that caused the death, must bear a reasonable relation to the kind of violence that constituted the provocation.

It is unnecessary for the purposes of the present appeal to spend time on a detailed account of what conduct was or was not capable in law of giving rise to a defence of provocation immediately before the passing of the Act of 1957 ... What, however, is important to note is that this House in *Holmes* v *DPP* [1946] AC 588 had recently confirmed that words alone, save perhaps in circumstances of a most extreme and exceptional nature, were incapable in law of constituting provocation.

My Lords, this was the state of law when *Bedder* v *DPP* [1959] 1 WLR 1119 fell to be considered by this House. The accused had killed a prostitute. He was sexually impotent. According to his evidence he had tried to have sexual intercourse with her and failed. She taunted him with his failure and tried to get away from his grasp. In the course of her attempts to do so she slapped him in the face, punched him in the stomach and kicked him in the groin, whereupon he took a knife out of his pocket and stabbed her twice and caused her death. The struggle that led to her death thus started because the deceased taunted the accused with his physical infirmity; but in the state of the law as it then was, taunts unaccompanied by any physical violence did not constitute provocation. The taunts were followed by violence on the part of the deceased in the course of her attempt to get away from the accused, and it may be that this subsequent violence would have a greater effect on the self-control of an impotent man already enraged by the taunts than it would have had upon a person conscious of possessing normal physical attributes. So there might have been some justification for the judge to instruct the jury to ignore the fact that the accused was impotent when they were considering whether the deceased's conduct amounted to such provocation as would cause a reasonable or ordinary person to lose his self control. This indeed appears to have been the ground on which the Court of Criminal Appeal had approved the summing-up when they said at p1121:

"... no distinction is to be made in the case of a person who, though it may not be a matter of temperament is physically impotent, is conscious of the impotence, *and therefore mentally liable to be more excited unduly* if he is 'twitted' or attacked on the subject of that particular infirmity."

This statement, for which I have myself supplied the emphasis, was approved by Lord Simonds LC speaking on behalf of all the members of this House who sat on the appeal; but he also went on to lay down the broader proposition at 1123, that:

"It would be plainly illogical not to recognise an unusually excitable or pugnacious temperament in the accused as a matter to be taken into account but yet to recognise for that purpose some unusual physical characteristic, be it impotence or another."

... My Lords, ... section [3] ... was intended to mitigate in some degree the harshness of the common law of provocation as it had been developed by recent decisions in this House. It recognises and retains the dual test: the provocation must not only have caused the accused to lose his self-control but also be such as might cause a reasonable man to react to it as the accused did. Nevertheless it brings about two important changes in the law. The first is it abolishes all previous rules of law as to what can or cannot amount to provocation and in particular the rule of law that, save in the two exceptional cases I have mentioned, words unaccompanied by violence could not do so. Secondly it makes clear that if there was any evidence that the accused himself at the time of the act which caused the death in fact lost his self-control in consequence of some provocation however slight it might appear to the judge, he was bound to leave to the jury the question, which is one of opinion not of law, whether a reasonable man might have reacted to that provocation as the accused did.

I agree with my noble and learned friend Lord Simon of Glaisdale that since this question is one for the opinion of the jury the evidence of witnesses as to how they think a reasonable man would react to the provocation is not admissible.

The public policy that underlay the adoption of the "reasonable man" test in the common law doctrine of provocation was to reduce the incidence of fatal violence by preventing a person relying on his own exceptional pugnacity or excitability as an excuse for loss of self-control. The rationale of the test may not be easy to reconcile in logic with more universal propositions as to the mental element in crime. Nevertheless it has been preserved by the Act of 1957 but falls to be applied now in the context of a law of provocation that is significantly different from what it was before the Act was passed.

Fagan v Metropolitan Police Commissioner [1969] 1 QB 439 Divisional Court (Lord Parker CJ, Bridge and James JJ)

Supervening fault

Facts

The defendant had been requested to park his car by the side of the road by a police constable. The defendant, in parking his car drove onto the police officer's foot. When the police officer requested that the defendant remove the car from his foot the defendant at first refused, using abusive language at the officer. After repeated requests the defendant removed the car. He was charged with assaulting a police officer in the execution of his duty. The defendant appealed on the ground that his driving of the car onto the police officer's foot could not have been an assault as he had done it accidentally. Further, allowing the car to remain on the police officer's foot could not constitute the assault, because assault required a positive act, whereas here there had been a failure to act.

Held

The appeal would be dismissed.

James J:

'In our judgment, the justices at Willesden and quarter sessions were right in law. On the facts found, the action of the appellant may have been initially unintentional, but the time came when, knowing that the wheel was on the officer's foot, the appellant (i) remained seated in the car so that his body through the medium of the car was in contact with the officer, (ii) switched off the ignition of the car, (iii) maintained the wheel of the car on the foot, and (iv) used words indicating the intention of keeping the wheel in that position. For our part, we cannot regard such conduct as mere omission or inactivity. There was an act constituting a battery which at its inception was not criminal because there was no element of intention, but which became criminal from the moment the intention was formed to produce the apprehension which was flowing from the continuing act. The fallacy of the appellant's argument is that it seeks to equate the facts of this case with such a case as where a motorist has accidentally run over a person and, that action having being completed, fails to assist the victim with the intent that the victim should suffer. We would dismiss this appeal.'

R v Bingham [1991] Crim LR 43 Court of Appeal (Criminal Division) (Lord Lane CJ, Henry and Hidden JJ)

Automatism - hypoglycaemia

Facts

D was arrested for shoplifting whilst in a hypoglycaemic state. The trial judge refused to allow him to put forward a defence of automatism based on his diabetes.

Held

Appeal allowed. Where there was sufficient evidence, a defence of automatism, based on the effects of insulin, should be allowed. The court noted, however, that where a diabetic was in a hyperglycaemic state due to lack of insulin, the possibility of a verdict of not guilty by reason of insanity arose.

R v Blaue (1975) 61 Cr App Rep 271 Court of Appeal (Criminal Division) (Lawton LJ, Thompson and Shaw JJ)

The 'thin skull' rule

Facts

The defendant stabbed the victim, who was a Jehovah's Witness, 13 times. She was rushed to hospital where doctors diagnosed that she would need an immediate blood transfusion if her life was to be saved. The victim refused the necessary transfusion because it was against her religious beliefs. She died from her wounds shortly after. The defendant appealed against his conviction for manslaughter on the ground that the refusal of treatment had broken the chain of causation.

Held

The appeal would be dismissed.

R v Byrne [1960] 2 QB 396 Court of Criminal Appeal (Parker CJ, Hilbury and Diplock JJ)

Abnormality of mind for purposes of diminished responsibility

Facts

The defendant had strangled a young woman. There was evidence that he was a sexual psychopath, and could exercise but little control over his actions. The defence of diminished responsibility was rejected by the trial judge, and the defendant was convicted of murder. He appealed on the basis that the defence should have been put to the jury.

Held

The appeal would be allowed, and a conviction for manslaughter substituted for murder, but the sentence of life imprisonment should remain.

Lord Parker CJ:

> 'In his summing-up the learned judge, after summarising the medical evidence, gave to the jury a direction of law on the correctness of which this appeal turns. He told the jury if on the evidence they came to the conclusion that the facts could be fairly summarised as follows: "(1) From an early age he has been subject to these perverted violent desires and in some cases has indulged his desires; (2) the impulse or urge of these desires is stronger than the normal impulse or urge of sex to such an extent that the subject finds it very difficult or perhaps impossible in some cases to resist putting the desire into practice; (3) the act of killing this girl was done under such an impulse or urge; and (4) that setting aside these sexual addictions and practices, this man was normal in every other respect," those facts with nothing more would not bring a case within the section and do not constitute such abnormality of mind as substantially to impair a man's mental responsibility for his acts. "In other words," he went on, "mental affliction is one thing. The section is there to protect them. The section is not there to give protection where there is nothing else than what is vicious and depraved." Taken by themselves, these last words are unobjectionable, but it is contended on behalf of the appellant that the direction taken as a whole involves a misconstruction of the section, and had the effect of withdrawing from the jury an issue of fact, which it was peculiarly their province to decide.

R v Cheshire (1991) 93 Cr App R 251 Court of Appeal (Criminal Division) (Beldam LJ, Boreham and Auld JJ)

Homicide - causation - inadequate medical treatment

Facts

The appellant fired two shots at the deceased (Trevor Jeffrey) during an argument at the Ozone fish and chip shop in Greenwich. The deceased received injuries to his leg and abdomen and died two months later in hospital. The appellant was convicted of murder and appealed on the ground that the trial judge had misdirected the jury on the issue of causation. The cause of the victim's death was given as 'cardio-respiratory arrest due to gunshot wounds', but the appellant had introduced expert evidence to the effect that the death had been caused by a rare complication resulting from the medical treatment he had received, and that the chain of causation had been broken by the negligent medical treatment. The trial judge had directed the jury that the medical treatment could not be regarded as a novus actus interveniens unless the doctors had been reckless in their disregard for the patient's health.

Held

The appeal would be dismissed.

Beldam LJ took, as his basis for the law relating to causation, the judgment of Goff LJ in *R v Pagett* (1983) 76 Cr App R 279.

He noted that while it was conceivable that acts or omissions of a doctor treating a victim injured by an accused could be so extraordinary that they could be regarded as independent of the accused's conduct, it was most unlikely that this would be the case.

In a situation such as this the court felt that the jury should be directed that they must be satisfied that the Crown has proved the death was caused by the acts of the accused - rather than necessarily being the sole or main cause of death, the accused's acts should have contributed significantly to the death.

Even where negligence of others was the immediate cause of the victim's death, the jury should not regard this as excluding responsibility on the part of the accused unless they regarded his acts as insignificant in causing the death, and the negligent treatment so independent of those acts and so potent in itself in causing the death.

It was not for the jury to weigh competing causes or to decide which was the dominant cause as long as they were satisfied that the accused's acts made a significant contribution to the death.

The rare complication which occurred in the victim's condition was a direct consequence of the appellant's acts; these remained a significant cause of the death.

R v Church [1966] 1 QB 59 Court of Criminal Appeal (Edmund-Davies, Marshall and Widgery JJ)

Nature of the dangerous unlawful act in constructive manslaughter

Facts

The defendant had gone to his van with the deceased, Mrs Nott, for sexual purposes. She had mocked his impotence and he had attacked her, knocking her out. The defendant panicked, and wrongly thinking he had killed her, threw her unconscious body into a river, where she drowned. The defendant appealed against his conviction for manslaughter.

Held

The appeal would be dismissed.

Edmund-Davies LJ:

> 'In the judgment of this court [the trial judge's direction on unlawful manslaughter] ... was a misdirection. It amounted to telling the jury that, whenever any unlawful act is committed in relation to a human being which resulted in death there must be, at least, a conviction for manslaughter. This might at one time have been regarded as good law: ... But it appears to this court that the passage of years has achieved a transformation in this branch of the law and, even in relation to manslaughter, a degree of mens rea has become recognised as essential ... [T]he conclusion of this court is that an unlawful act causing the death of another cannot, simply because it is an unlawful act, render a manslaughter verdict inevitable. For such a verdict inexorably to follow, the unlawful act must be such as all sober and reasonable people would inevitably recognise must subject the other person to, at least, the risk of some harm resulting therefrom, albeit not serious harm ...'

R v Cunningham [1957] 2 QB 396 Court of Criminal Appeal (Byrne, Slade, and Barry JJ)

Subjective recklessness

Facts

The defendant had entered the basement of a building and ripped a gas meter from the wall in order to remove the money that it contained. In his efforts the defendant ruptured the gas supply pipes with the result that gas escaped and seeped through the porous basement wall into an adjoining property, which was occupied by a Mrs Wade and her husband. The defendant was convicted of maliciously administering a noxious substance, contrary to s23 of the Offences Against the Person Act 1861, following a direction from the trial judge that the jury were to convict if they were satisfied that the defendant's action had been 'wicked'. The defendant appealed to the Court of Appeal.

Held

The appeal would be allowed.

Byrne J:

> '... the following principle which was propounded by the late Professor CS Kenny in the first edition of his Outlines of Criminal Law published in 1902 and repeated in 1952: "In any statutory definition of a crime, malice must be taken not in the old vague sense of wickedness in general but as requiring either (1) An actual intention to do the particular kind of harm that in fact was done; or (2) recklessness as to whether such harm should occur or not (ie, the accused has foreseen that the particular kind of harm might be done and yet has gone on to take the risk of it). It is neither limited to nor does it indeed require any ill will towards the person injured." The same principle is repeated by Mr Turner in his 10th edition of Russell on Crime at p1592.
>
> We think that this is an accurate statement of the law. It derives some support from the judgments of Lord Coleridge CJ and Blackburn J in *Pembliton's Case* (1874) LR 2 CCR 119. In our opinion the word "maliciously" in a statutory crime postulates foresight of the consequence ...'

R v Dudley and Stephens (1884) 14 QBD 273 Queen's Bench Division (Lord Coleridge CJ, Grove and Denman JJ, Pollock and Huddlestone BB)

Availability of the defence of necessity

Facts

The two defendants, a third man and a cabin boy, were cast adrift in a boat following a shipwreck. They were 1600 miles from land, and had endured seven days without food and water, when the defendants decided to kill the cabin boy, who was in any case close to death, so that they might eat his flesh and drink his blood, in the hope that they might then survive long enough to be rescued. Four days after the killing, the three survivors were picked up by a passing vessel. On returning to England the defendants were charged with the boy's murder. The jury returned a special verdict whereby they found that, although the defendants would probably not have survived had they not killed the boy, and that he was likely to have died first anyway, there was no greater necessity for killing the boy than any of the other survivors. The jury's finding was referred to the judges of the Queen's Bench Division.

Held

The defendants could not raise the defence of necessity to a charge of murder.

Lord Coleridge CJ:

> 'Now, except for the purpose of testing how far the conservation of a man's own life is in all cases and under all circumstances, an absolute, unqualified, and paramount duty, we exclude from our consideration all the incidents of war. We are dealing with a case of private homicide, not one imposed upon men in the service of their Sovereign and in the defence of their country. Now it is admitted that the deliberate killing of this unoffending and unresisting boy was clearly murder, unless the killing can be justified by some well-recognised excuse admitted by the law. It is further admitted that there was in this case no such excuse, unless the killing was justified by what has been called "necessity". But the temptation to the act which existed here was not what the law has ever called necessity. Nor is this to be regretted. Though law and morality are not the same, and many things may be immoral which are not necessarily illegal, yet the absolute divorce of law from morality would be of fatal consequence; and such divorce would follow if the temptation to murder in this case

were to be held by law an absolute defence of it. It is not so. To preserve one's life is generally speaking a duty, but it may be the plainest and the highest duty to sacrifice it. War is full of instances in which it is a man's duty not to live, but to die. The duty, in case of shipwreck, of a captain to his crew, of the crew to the passengers, of soldiers to women and children, as in the noble case of *The Birkenhead*; these duties impose on men the moral necessity, not of the preservation, but of the sacrifice of their lives for others, from which in no country, least of all, it is to be hoped, in England, will men ever shrink, as indeed they have not shrunk.'

R v Dyson [1908] 2 KB 454 Court of Criminal Appeal

Year and a day rule

Facts

The defendant assaulted his own child causing a fractured skull in November 1906. The child died in March 1908, the medical evidence being that the fractured skull was the main cause of death. The defendant was convicted of manslaughter and appealed.

Held

The conviction would be quashed, because of misdirection by the trial judge to the jury.

R v Ghosh (1982) 75 Cr App R 154 Court of Appeal (Criminal Division) (Lord Lane CJ, Lloyd and Eastham JJ)

Direction to the jury on dishonesty

Facts

As stated by Lord Lane CJ:

'On 29 April 1981 before the Crown Court in St Albans, the appellant was convicted on four counts of an indictment laid under the Theft Act 1968: on count 1, attempting to procure the execution of a cheque by deception; on count 2, attempting to obtain money by deception; on counts 3 and 4, obtaining money by deception. Count 1 was laid under section 20(2) and the remainder under section 15(1). He was fined the sum of £250 on each count with a term of imprisonment to be served in default of payment.

At all material times the appellant was a surgeon acting as a *locum tenens* consultant at a hospital. The charges alleged that he had falsely represented that he had himself carried out a surgical operation to terminate pregnancy or that money was due to himself or an anaesthetist for such an operation, when in fact the operation had been carried out by someone else, and/or under the National Health Service provisions.

His defence was that there was no deception; that the sums paid to him were due for consultation fees which were legitimately payable under the regulations, or else were the balance of fees properly payable; in other words that there was nothing dishonest about his behaviour on any of the counts.

The effect of the jury's verdict was as follows: as to count 1, that the appellant had falsely represented that he had carried out a surgical operation and had intended dishonestly to obtain money thereby; that as to count 2 he had falsely pretended that an operation had been carried out under the National Health Service; that as to count 3 he had falsely pretended that money was due to an anaesthetist; and as to count 4 that he had obtained money by falsely pretending that an operation had been carried out on a fee-paying basis when in fact it had been conducted under the terms of the National Health Service.

The grounds of appeal are simply that the learned judge misdirected the jury as to the meaning of dishonestly.'

Held

The appeal would be dismissed.

Lord Lane CJ:

> 'So far as the present case is concerned, it seems to us that once the jury had rejected the defendant's account in respect of each count in the indictment (as they plainly did) the finding of dishonesty was inevitable, whichever of the tests of dishonesty was applied. If the judge had asked the jury to determine whether the defendant might have believed that what he did was in accordance with the ordinary man's idea of honesty, there could have only been one answer - and that is no, once the jury had rejected the defendant's explanation of what happened.
>
> In so far as there was a misdirection on the meaning of dishonesty, it is plainly a case for the application of the proviso to section 2(1) of the Act. This appeal is accordingly dismissed.'

R v Holden [1991] Crim LR 478 Court of Appeal (Criminal Division) (Mustill LJ, Tudor Evans and Thorpe JJ)

Dishonesty in theft

Facts

D was charged with theft of scrap tyres from Kwik Fit where he was an employee. He claimed he had seen others taking home scrap tyres and thought it was permitted. The trial judge directed the jury that his belief that it was permitted had to be honest and reasonable.

Held

Under s2(1)(a) of the Theft Act 1968, the defendant merely had to show that he honestly believed he had the right to take the property. The appeal would be allowed.

R v Jordan (1956) 40 Cr App R 152 Court of Criminal Appeal (Hallett, Ormrod and Donovan JJ)

Medical treatment as a novus actus interveniens

Facts

The defendant had stabbed the victim, a man named Beaumont, who was admitted to hospital where he died some eight days later. The defendant was convicted of murder, but appealed when new evidence came to light that the victim had been given a drug whilst in hospital to which he was allergic.

Held

The conviction would be quashed.

Hallett J:

> '... We are disposed to accept it as the law that death resulting from any normal treatment employed to deal with a felonious injury may be regarded as caused by the felonious injury, but we do not think it necessary to examine the cases in detail or to formulate for the assistance of those who have to deal with such matters in the future the correct test which ought to be laid down with regard to what is necessary to be proved in order to establish causal connection between the death and the felonious injury. Not only one feature, but two separate and independent features, of treatment were, in the opinion of the doctors, palpably wrong and these produced the symptoms discovered at the post-mortem examination which were the direct and immediate cause of death, namely, the pneumonia resulting from the condition of oedema which was found.'

R v Larsonneur (1933) 149 LT 542 Court of Criminal Appeal (Lord Hewart CJ, Avory and Humphreys JJ)

Absence of a freely willed actus reus: absolute liability

Facts

The defendant, a French national, entered the United Kingdom lawfully, but was given only a restricted power to remain in the country. Her passport stated that she had to leave the United Kingdom on 22 March 1933. On that day the defendant left England, not to return to France, but to travel to the Irish Free State. The Irish authorities made a deportation order against her, and she was forcibly removed from Ireland and returned to the United Kingdom mainland at Holyhead. On arrival at Holyhead the defendant was charged, under the Aliens Order 1920, with 'being found' in the United Kingdom whilst not having permission to enter the country. The defendant was convicted, and appealed on the basis that her return to the United Kingdom had not been of her own free will, in that she had been forcibly taken to Holyhead by the immigration authorities.

Held

The appeal would be dismissed.

R v Lawrence [1982] AC 510 House of Lords (Lords Hailsham, Diplock, Fraser, Roskill and Bridge)

Objective recklessness

Facts

The defendant motor cyclist had collided with and killed a pedestrian. He was convicted of causing death by reckless driving contrary to s1 of the Road Traffic Act 1972. The conviction was quashed by the Court of Appeal, and the prosecution appealed to the House of Lords.

Held

The appeal would be dismissed.

Lord Diplock:

'My Lords, this House has very recently had occasion in *R* v *Caldwell* [1982] AC 341 to give close consideration to the concept of recklessness as constituting mens rea in criminal law. The conclusion reached by the majority was that the adjective "reckless" when used in criminal statute, ie the Criminal Damage Act 1971, had not acquired a special meaning as a term of legal art, but bore its popular or dictionary meaning of careless, regardless, or heedless of the possible harmful consequences of one's act. The same must be true of the adverbial derivative "recklessly".

The context in which the word "reckless" appears in section 1 of the Criminal Damage Act 1971 differs in two respects from the context in which the word "recklessly" appears in sections 1 and 2 of the Road Traffic Act 1972 as now amended. In the Criminal Damage Act 1971 the actus reus, the physical act of destroying or damaging property belonging to another, is in itself a tort. It is not something that one does regularly as part of the ordinary routine of daily life, such as driving a car or a motor cycle. So there is something out of the ordinary to call the doer's attention to what he is doing and its possible consequences, which is absent in road traffic offences. The other difference in context is that in section 1 of the Criminal Damage Act 1971 the mens rea of the offences is defined as being reckless as to whether particular harmful consequences would occur, whereas in sections 1 and 2 of the Road Traffic Act 1972, as now amended, the possible harmful consequences of which the driver must be shown to have been heedless are left to be implied from the use of the word "recklessly" itself. In ordinary usage "recklessly" as descriptive of a physical act such as driving a motor vehicle which can be performed in a variety of different ways, some of them entailing danger and some of them not, refers not only to the state of mind of the doer of the act when he decides to do it but also qualifies the manner in which the act itself is performed. One does not speak of a person acting "recklessly", even though he has given no thought at all to the consequences of his act, unless the act is one that presents a real risk of harmful consequences which anyone acting with reasonable prudence would recognise and give heed to. So the actus reus of the offences under sections 1 and 2 is not simply driving a motor vehicle on a road, but driving it in a manner which in fact creates a real risk of harmful consequences resulting from it.

R v Morris; Anderton v Burnside (Consolidated Appeals) [1983] 3 WLR 697 House of Lords (Lords Fraser, Edmund-Davies, Roskill, Brandon and Brightman)

Appropriation - whether an unauthorised act required

Facts

As stated by Lord Roskill:

'Morris, the appellant from the Court of Appeal (Criminal Division), on 30 October 1981, took goods from the shelves of a supermarket. He replaced the price labels attached to them with labels showing a lesser price than the originals. At the checkout point he was asked for and paid those lesser prices. He was then arrested. Burnside, the appellant from the Division Court, was seen to remove a price label from a joint of pork in the supermarket and attach it to a second joint. This action was detected at the checkout point but before he had paid for that second joint which at that moment bore a price label showing a price of £2.73 whereas the label should have shown a price of £6.91 1/2. Burnside was then arrested.

The only relevant difference between the two cases is that Burnside was arrested before he had dishonestly paid the lesser price for the joint of pork. Morris was arrested after he had paid the relevant lesser prices. Morris was tried in Acton Crown Court on two charges of theft contrary to section 1(1) of the Theft Act 1968. A third count of obtaining property by deception contrary to section 15 of that Act appeared in the indictment but the learned assistant recorder did not take a verdict upon it and ordered that count to remain on the file. Morris appealed. The Court of Appeal (Criminal Division) (Lord Lane CJ, O'Connor LJ and Talbot J) dismissed his appeal in a reserved judgment given on 8 March 1983, by the learned Lord Chief Justice.

Burnside was convicted at Manchester Magistrates' Court on 27 January 1982, on a single charge of theft contrary to section 1(1) of the Theft Act. He appealed by way of case stated. On 5 November 1982, the Divisional Court (Ackner LJ and Webster J) dismissed the appeal.

Both the Court of Appeal (Criminal Division) and the Divisional Court granted certificates. The former certificate read thus: "If a person has substituted on an item of goods displayed in a self-service store a price label showing a lesser price for one showing a greater price, with the intention of paying the lesser price and then pays the lesser price at the till and takes the goods, is there at any stage a 'dishonest appropriation' for the purposes of section 1 of the Theft Act 1968 and if so, at what point does such appropriation take place?"

The certificate in the latter case reads: "If a person has substituted on an item of goods displayed in a self-service store a price label showing a lesser price for one showing a greater price, with the intention of paying the lesser price, and then pays the lesser price at the till and takes the goods, is there at any stage a 'dishonest appropriation' for the purposes of section 1 of the Theft Act 1968?"

The two certificates though clearly intended to raise the same point of law are somewhat differently worded and, with respect, as both learned counsel ultimately accepted during the debate before your Lordships, do not precisely raise the real issue for decision, at least in the terms in which it falls to be decided.'

Held

The appeals would be dismissed.

R v Seers [1985] Crim LR 315 Court of Appeal (Criminal Division) (Griffiths LJ, Stocker J, and Sir John Thompson)

Diminished responsibility distinguished from insanity

Facts

The appellant stabbed and killed his wife outside the hostel in which she had been staying and was subsequently charged with murder. At the trial he pleaded guilty to manslaughter, but not guilty to murder, raising the defences of provocation, and diminished responsibility under section 2 of the Homicide Act 1957.

On the latter issue, medical evidence was called by both sides, the defence calling the prison medical officer, the prosecution a consultant psychiatrist. Both doctors agreed that the appellant was suffering from chronic reactive depression, which the appellant argued amounted to a mental illness giving rise to an abnormality of mind of a degree which substantially impaired his mental responsibility at the time of the killing. Both doctors agreed that a reactive depressive illness could amount to such an abnormality of mind, but differed as to whether, in this case, it had in fact done so.

The judge directed the jury that the test to be applied to determine whether Seers' responsibility was diminished was whether he could be described in popular language as partially insane or on the borderline of insanity. Both doctors had been asked whether this description could be applied to the appellant, and both agreed that it could not.

On appeal, it was argued that reference to borderline or partial insanity was not an appropriate test in this type of case, certainly not as the sole test to be applied: the judge should have directed the jury to consider whether the defendant's ability to control his hostility towards his wife had been substantially impaired by a depressive illness.

Held (and substituting a conviction for manslaughter instead of murder)

There had been a substantial misdirection on the issue of diminished responsibility. *R v Byrne* (1960) 44 Cr App R 246 ought not to be read as laying down that in every case where diminished responsibility is raised the jury must necessarily be directed that the test is always to be partial or borderline insanity. There may be cases where the abnormality of mind may not be readily relatable to any of the generally recognised types of insanity in the broad popular sense. There is no one safe formula for directing the jury: the direction must always be related to the particular evidence in the case (*R v Rose* (1961) 45 Cr App R 102 applied).

In a case of this sort, dealing with a depressive illness, it is not appropriate to direct a jury solely (or, semble, at all) in terms of partial or borderline insanity as the test of diminished responsibility (*Byrne*, supra, distinguished as a case where the evidence of doctors, who agreed that Byrne, a sexual psychopath could be described as partially insane, justified inviting the jury to determine the degree of impairment of mental responsibility by such a test).

Sentence of eight years' imprisonment substituted.

R v Smith [1959] 2 QB 35 Courts-Martial Appeal Court (Lord Parker CJ, Streatfield and Hinchcliffe JJ)

Homicide - causation in law

Facts

The defendant had been involved in a barrack room fight with a fellow soldier, Private Creed. During the course of the fight the defendant had stabbed the victim several times with a bayonet, and the victim was taken to a medical post where he died approximately one hour later. The defendant contended that the chain of causation between the stabbing and the death had been broken by the way in which the victim had been treated, in particular the fact that he had been handled roughly whilst being carried to the medical post, and the delay in providing him with treatment once he arrived there because of the number of other cases being dealt with. The defendant was convicted of murder and appealed.

Held

The appeal would be dismissed, the chain of causation not having been broken by the intervening events.

R v Tolson (1889) 23 QBD 168 Court for Crown Cases Reserved (Lord Coleridge CJ, Denman, Field, Manisty, Hawkins, Stephen, Cave, Day, A L Smith, Wills, Grantham and Charles JJ, Pollock and Huddleston BB)

Mistake as a defence to crimes of strict liability

Facts

The defendant was deserted by her husband in 1881. She was subsequently told by her brother-in-law that he had drowned at sea. In 1887, honestly (although mistakenly) believing herself to be a widow, the defendant remarried. In December 1887 the defendant's husband returned from America, and she was convicted of bigamy contrary to s58 of the Offences Against the Person Act 1861. Her appeal was considered by the Court for Crown Cases Reserved.

Held

(By a majority of nine to five) the conviction would be quashed.

Stephen J:

> 'My view of the subject is based upon a particular application of the doctrine usually, though I think not happily, described by the phrase "non est reus, nisi mens set rea." ... The principle involved appears to me, when fully considered, to amount to no more than this. The full definition of every crime contains expressly or by implication a proposition as to a state of mind. Therefore, if the mental element of any conduct alleged to be a crime is proved to have been absent in any given case, the crime so defined is not committed; or, again if a crime is fully defined, nothing amounts to that crime which does not satisfy that definition. Crimes are in the present day much more accurately defined by statute or otherwise than they formerly were. The mental element of most crimes is marked by one of the words "maliciously," "fraudulently," "negligently," or "knowingly," but it is the general - I might, I think, say, the invariable - practice of the legislature to leave unexpressed some of the mental elements of crime. In all cases whatever, competent age, sanity and some degree of freedom from some kinds of coercion are assumed to be essential to criminality, but I do not believe they are ever introduced into any statute by which any particular crime is defined.
>
> The meaning of the words "malice," "negligence" and "fraud" in relation to particular crimes has been ascertained by numerous cases. Malice means one thing in relation to murder, another in relation to the Malicious Mischief Act, and a third in relation to libel, and so of fraud and negligence.
>
> With regard to knowledge of fact, the law, perhaps, is not quite so clear, but it may, I think, be maintained that in every case knowledge of fact is to some extent an element of criminality as much as competent age and sanity. To take an extreme illustration, can anyone doubt that a man who, though he might be perfectly sane, committed what would otherwise be a crime in a state of somnambulism, would be entitled to be acquitted? And why is this? Simply because he would not know what he was doing.

R v Williams; R v Davies (1991) The Times 23 October Court of Appeal (Criminal Division) (Stuart-Smith LJ, Waterhouse and Morland JJ)

Homicide - causation - victim's escape

Facts

Williams was the driver of a car which had stopped to give a lift to the deceased, a man called Shephard. Five miles further on, Shephard jumped out of the car whilst it was travelling at 30 miles per hour and suffered fatal head injuries. The evidence indicated that Williams had asked Shephard to make a contribution to the cost of petrol. Davis, also a passenger in the car, alleged that Williams had threatened Shephard with violence if he did not hand over the money, with the result that Shephard had jumped from the car whilst it was moving. Williams contended that Shephard had jumped out following threats made by Davis. In Davis's case, the trial judge had dealt with the issue of causation by directing the jury on the basis of *DPP* v *Daley* (1979) 69 Cr App R 39, which appeared to establish six criteria for proof of causation in so-called 'escape' cases:

i) that the victim, immediately before sustaining the injuries was in fear of being hurt physically;

ii) that the victim's fear was such that it caused him to escape;

iii) that the victim met his death because of his attempts to escape, and in the course of trying to escape;

iv) that the victim's fear of being hurt was reasonable and could be related to the actions of the accused;

v) that the fear was caused by an unlawful act committed by the accused;

vi) that the accused's conduct was such that a sober and reasonable person would foresee it as likely to subject the victim to a risk of some harm, albeit not serious.

Davis was convicted of manslaughter and robbery, and appealed on the ground that the trial judge's direction on causation had been inadequate.

Held

The appeal would be allowed. The *Daley* guidelines were inappropriate where there was a real issue as to causation, as in cases where the victim was frightened into making an escape. The jury should be directed to consider whether it was reasonably foreseeable that some harm, albeit not serious harm, was likely to result from the threat made. Further, the jury should be directed to consider whether the response of the victim was within the scope of reasonably foreseeable responses that might be expected from a victim in that particular situation.

Shaw v DPP [1962] AC 220 House of Lords (Viscount Simmonds, Lords Reid, Tucker, Morris of Borth-y-Gest and Hodson)

Creation of new offence by the judiciary: policy considerations in judicial law making

Facts

The appellant published a circular known as the 'Ladies Directory' which was in effect a 'contact magazine' for prostitutes and their potential clients. He was convicted, inter alia, for conspiring to corrupt public morals. He appealed unsuccessfuly to the Court of Appeal on the ground that there was no such offence known to law. He appealed further to the House of Lords.

Held (Lord Reid dissenting)

The appeal would be dismissed.

See also Chapter 1.

Sherras v De Rutzen [1895] 1 QB 918 Divisional Court (Day and Wright JJ)

Imposition of strict liability

Facts

The defendant was convicted of selling alcohol to a police officer whilst on duty, contrary to s16(2) of the Licensing Act 1872. He appealed to the Divisional Court on the ground that he could not have known that the police officer was on duty as he had not been wearing the arm band that would have indicated this.

Held

The conviction would be quashed.

Wright J:

'There is a presumption that mens rea, an evil intention, or a knowledge of the wrongfulness of the act, is an essential ingredient in every offence; but that presumption is liable to be displaced either by the words of the statute creating the offence or by the subject-matter with which it deals, and both must be considered: *Nichols* v *Hall* (1873) LR 8 CP 322. One of the most remarkable exceptions was in the case of bigamy. It is plain that if guilty knowledge is not necessary, no care on the part of the publican could save him from a conviction under section 16, subsection (2), since it would be as easy for the constable to deny that he was on duty when asked, or to produce a forged permission from his superior officer, as to remove his armlet before entering the public-house. I am, therefore, of opinion that this conviction ought to be quashed.'

Thabo Meli v R [1954] 1 WLR 228 Privy Council (Lord Goddard CJ, Lord Reid and Mr LMD de Silva)

Coincidence of actus reus and mens rea

Facts

The defendants took their intended victim to a hut and plied him with drink so that he became intoxicated, they then hit the victim around the head, intending to kill him. In fact the defendants only succeeded in knocking him unconscious, but believing him to be dead, they threw the victim's body over a cliff. The victim died some time later of exposure. The defendants were convicted of murder, and appealed to the Privy Council on the ground that there was no coincidence of the mens rea and actus reus of murder. The defendants' submissions were that when they had acted with the intention of killing the victim by striking him on the head, they had failed to kill him. On the other hand, when they did actually cause his death, by throwing him over the cliff, they lacked the mens rea for murder as they believed he was already dead.

Held

The appeal would be dismissed. The correct view of what the defendants had done was to treat the chain of events as a continuing actus reus. The actus reus of causing death started with the victim being struck on the head and continued until he died of exposure. It was sufficient for the prosecution to establish that at some time during that chain of events the defendants had acted with the requisite mens rea for murder.

3 LAW OF TORT

American Cyanamid Co v Ethicon [1975] AC 396; [1975] 2 WLR 316
See Chapters 1 and 4.

Balfour v Balfour [1919] 2 KB 571
See Chapter 4.

Blyth v Birmingham Waterworks Co (1856) 11 Exch 781 Court of Exchequer (Alderson, Martin and Bramwell BB)
Negligence - frost of exceptional severity

Facts

In pursuance of statutory powers, the defendants laid down water pipes. During 'one of the severest frosts on record', a plug failed to work correctly and a large quantity of water escaped into the plaintiff's house.

Held

On the facts, the defendants were not liable.

Alderson B:

> 'The case turns upon the question whether the facts proved show that the defendants were guilty of negligence. Negligence is the omission to do something which a reasonable man, guided upon those considerations which ordinarily regulate the conduct of human affairs, would do, or doing something which a prudent and reasonable man would not do. The defendants might have been liable for negligence, if, unintentionally, they omitted to do that which a reasonable person would have done, or did that which a person taking reasonable precautions would not have done. A reasonable man would act with reference to the average circumstances of the temperature in ordinary years. The defendants had provided against such frosts as experience would have led men, acting prudently, to provide against; and they are not guilty of negligence, because their precautions proved insufficient against the effects of the extreme severity of the frost of 1855, which penetrated to a greater depth than any which ordinarily occurs south of the polar regions. Such a state of circumstances constitutes a contingency against which no reasonable man can provide. The result was an accident, for which the defendants cannot be held liable.'

Bolton v Stone [1951] AC 850 House of Lords (Lords Porter, Normand, Oaksey, Reid and Radcliffe)
Negligence - injury from cricket ball

Facts

The plaintiff was standing on the highway when she was hit by a cricket ball which had been struck from the defendant's adjoining cricket ground. The evidence showed that, in the many years that cricket had been played on the ground, only very occasionally had the ball been hit so far. The ball had travelled over 100 yards after being hit and had cleared a seven-foot boundary fence. The plaintiff sued in, inter alia, negligence. In the House of Lords it was conceded that, in the circumstances, nuisance could not be established unless negligence was proved.

Held

The defendants were not negligent in failing to take steps to guard against such a small risk: such an injury would not have been anticipated by a reasonable man.

Lord Oaksey:

> 'An ordinary, careful man does not take precautions against every foreseeable risk. He can, of course, foresee the possibility of many risks, but life would be almost impossible if he were to attempt to take precautions against every risk which he can foresee. He takes precautions against risks which are reasonably likely to happen.'

Lord Reid:

> 'In the crowded conditions of modern life, even the most careful person cannot avoid creating some risks and accepting others. What a man must not do ... is to create a risk which is substantial.'

British Railways Board v Herrington [1972] AC 877 House of Lords (Lords Reid, Morris of Borth-y-Gest, Wilberforce, Pearson and Diplock)

Negligence - duty owed to trespasser

The respondent, a six year old boy, was playing in a field beside which ran the appellants' railway line. The fence between the field and the line was in a bad state of repair and in fact, people often broke through it to cross the railway line. Some weeks before the appellants had been told of the presence of children on the line. The respondent passed through the fence and was electrocuted on the live rail.

Held

The appellants owed the respondent a duty of common humanity and though he was a trespasser, he was entitled to recover damages.

Byrne v Deane [1937] 1 KB 818 Court of Appeal (Greer, Slesser and Greene LJJ)

Libel - report to police

Facts

For many years gambling machines had been installed in the local golf club. Someone informed the police. The machines were removed and a notice appeared on the board, saying:

> 'He who gave the game away, may he byrne in hell and rue the day.'

The plaintiff brought an action in libel, saying that the words implied he had reported the matter to the police and was guilty of underhand disloyalty to the defendant club proprietors and fellow members.

Held

The words were not defamatory as it is not defamatory to say of someone that he has reported a crime to the police.

Slesser LJ:

> 'We have to consider in this connection the arbitrium boni, the view which would be taken by the ordinary good and worthy subject of the King ... such a good and worthy subject would not consider such an allegation in itself to be defamatory.'

Christie v Davey [1893] 1 Ch 316 High Court (North J)

Nuisance - 'retaliation'

The plaintiff was a music teacher living with her husband, daughter (who studied at the Royal Academy of Music and was also a teacher) and a lodger friend of the daughter with like qualifications. The son of the house played the cello (badly!). The defendant lived next door and wrote to the plaintiff, requesting that the amount of music played be curbed. When he received no reply, the defendant commenced 'retaliation' by shrieking, banging and howling. This disrupted the plaintiff's professional music lessons and she sued for an injunction, claiming the retaliation amounted to nuisance.

Held

While the playing of music was not here a nuisance, the defendant's behaviour did amount to a nuisance and it would be restrained by injunction.

North J:

'If what has taken place had occurred between two sets of persons both perfectly innocent, I should have taken an entirely different view of the case. But, I am persuaded that what was done by the defendant was done solely for the purpose of annoyance and, in any view, it was not a legitimate use of the defendant's house.'

D & F Estates Ltd v Church Commissioners for England [1988] 3 WLR 368 House of Lords (Lords Bridge of Harwich, Templeman, Ackner, Oliver of Aylmerton and Jauncey of Tullichettle)

Negligence - extent of duty - economic loss

Facts

The third defendants (Wates) were the main contractors for the construction of a block of flats (Chelwood House) owned by the first defendants: they engaged a sub-contractor, whom they reasonably believed to be skilled and competent, to carry out the plastering, but he did the work negligently. Some 15 years after construction, and again some three years later, the plaintiffs, lessees and occupiers of one of the flats, found that the plaster in their flat was loose; they sued, inter alia, Wates, claiming the cost of remedial work already carried out and the estimated cost of future remedial work.

Held

Their claim could not succeed as (a) it was for pure economic loss and (b) Wates' only duty was to engage a competent contractor which they had done.

Donoghue (or McAlister) v Stevenson [1932] AC 562 House of Lords (Lord Buckmaster, Lord Atkin, Lord Tomlin, Lord Thankerton and Lord Macmillan)

Negligence - duty of care

Facts

The appellant went, together with her friend, to a cafe, where the friend purchased a bottle of ginger beer which was sealed and in opaque glass. Both drank from the ginger beer before realising that it contained a dead snail. The appellant suffered gastro-enteritis and shock as a result and sued the manufacturer of the ginger beer for damages on the ground that he had been negligent in the production of the product. The only question before the House of Lords was whether the respondent (manufacturer) owed a duty of care to the appellant.

Held (Lord Buckmaster and Lord Tomlin dissenting)

The respondent owed the appellant a duty of care, although he did not know the product to be dangerous and no contractual relationship existed between the parties. On proof of the facts the appellant would be entitled to damages.

Lord Atkin:

'You must take reasonable care to avoid acts or omissions which you can reasonably foresee would be likely to injure your neighbour. Who then, in law, is my neighbour? The answer seems to be - persons who are so closely and directly affected by my act that I ought reasonably to have them in contemplation as being so affected when I am directing my mind to the acts or omission which are called in question.'

Lord Macmillan:

'In the daily contacts of social and business life, human beings are thrown into, or place themselves in, an infinite variety of relations with their fellows; and the law can refer only to the standards of the reasonable man in order to determine whether any particular relation gives rise to a duty to take care, as between those who stand in that relation to each other. The grounds of action may be as various and manifold as human errancy; and the conception of legal responsibility may develop in adaptation to altering social conditions and standards. The criterion of judgment must adjust and adapt itself to the changing circumstances of life. The categories of negligence are never closed.'

Heasmans v Clarity Cleaning Co Ltd [1987] ICR 949 Court of Appeal (Purchas and Nourse LJJ)

Vicarious liability - conversion

Facts

An office cleaning contractor company employed a cleaning lady whose task it was to go into offices after hours and clean the offices. Whilst in the office she used the telephone to make personal calls (adding up to £1,500 in total). The plaintiffs, the owner of the office, sued the defendant, the contractor, as being vicariously liable for the conversion of the cleaning lady.

Held

The defendants were not vicariously liable for the cleaning lady's phone calls. They were not made in the course of employment, as phoning was not part of her duties, though cleaning the phone was.

Hedley Byrne & Co Ltd v Heller & Partners [1964] AC 465 House of Lords (Lords Reid, Morris of Borth-y-Gest, Hodson, Devlin and Pearce)

Negligence - duty of care in relation to information or advice

Facts

The appellants, an advertising agency, wished to make enquiries about the financial reliability of one of their customers, Easipower Ltd. Their bankers made enquiries of the respondents, Easipower's bankers. The respondents replied, first orally then in writing, stating that Easipower Ltd was financially sound, although this information was given 'without responsibility'. The appellants relied on this advice which proved to be inaccurate and they suffered considerable losses when Easipower went into liquidation.

Held

A duty of care in making statements may arise when the parties are in a 'special relationship'. But the appeal was dismissed because the respondents had excluded their responsibility.

See also Chapter 4.

Holliday v National Telephone Co [1899] 2 QB 392 Court of Appeal (Earl of Halsbury LC, A L Smith and Vaughan Williams LJJ)

Negligence - independent contractor

Facts

When laying telephone wires in trenches under a highway, the defendants engaged a plumber - an independent contractor - to carry out some aspects of the work. Due to the negligence of the plumber's employee, there was an explosion and molten solder flew out and injured the plaintiff who was passing along the footway.

Held

The defendants were liable.

A L Smith LJ:

> 'Where a person is executing work upon a public highway, he cannot escape liability by employing an independent contractor, because there is a duty cast upon him to see that the work upon the highway is so carried out as not to injure persons who are using the highway.'

Honeywill & Stein Ltd v Larkin Bros (London's Commercial Photographers) Ltd [1934] 1 KB 191 Court of Appeal (Lord Hewart CJ, Lord Wright and Slessor LJ)

Independent contractor - negligence

Facts

After they had installed sound reproduction apparatus in a cinema, the plaintiffs employed the defendants to take photograph of the cinema's interior. The defendants negligently set light to the cinema's curtains and the plaintiffs sought to recover from the defendants the compensation which they (the plaintiffs) had paid to the cinema's owners.

Held

They should succeed as they were themselves liable to the cinema owners for the defendant's negligence.

Slessor LJ:

> 'To take a photograph in the cinema with a flashlight was, on the evidence stated above, a dangerous operation in its intrinsic nature, involving the creation of fire and explosion on another person's premises, that is, in the cinema, the property of the cinema company. The plaintiffs, in procuring this work to be performed by their contractors, the defendants, assumed an obligation to the cinema company which was, as we think, absolute, but which was at least an obligation to use reasonable precautions to see that no damage resulted to the cinema company from those dangerous operations. That obligation they could not delegate by employing the defendants as independent contractors, but they were liable in this regard for the defendants' acts. For the damage actually caused the plaintiffs were, accordingly, liable in law to the cinema company, and are entitled to claim and recover from the defendants damages for their breach of contract or negligence in performing their contract to take photographs.'

Lim Poh Choo v Camden & Islington Area Health Authority [1980] AC 174

See Chapter 1.

Lister v Romford Ice & Cold Storage Co [1957] AC 555

See Chapter 1.

McWilliams (or Cummings) v Sir William Arrol & Co Ltd [1962] 1 WLR 295 House of Lords (Viscount Kilmuir LC, Viscount Simonds, Lords Reid, Morris of Borth-y-Gest and Devlin)

Negligence - causation

Facts

The plaintiff was the widow of a steel erector who was employed by the defendants. On one occasion when he was erecting a steel tower some seventy feet from the ground, he slipped and fell to his death. His widow alleged the defendants were at fault in not providing safety belts, an item which clearly would have saved the deceased. The defendants alleged that, although such belts were customary, even if they had provided one, there was a high degree of probability that the deceased would not have worn it and that, therefore, any breach of duty on their part was not the cause of the deceased's death.

Held

The plaintiff's claim failed as the defendants' breach of duty (if there was one) was not the cause of the accident since (a) on the evidence the deceased would not have worn a safety belt if it had been provided and (b) there was no duty on the defendants to instruct or exhort the deceased to wear a safety belt.

Mersey Docks & Harbour Board v Coggins & Griffith (Liverpool) Ltd [1947] AC 1 House of Lords (Viscount Simon, Lords Macmillan, Porter, Simonds and Uthwatt)

Vicarious liability - employee on loan

Facts

M1 hired to M2 a crane and driver. Whilst on hire, M1 was responsible for paying the driver and could dismiss him, but the hire agreement declared the driver to be M2's employee. Due to the driver's negligence in operating the crane, one of M2's employees was injured. Was M1 or M2 vicariously liable?

Held

M1, being the permanent employer, retained control over the driver and was vicariously liable.

Lord Porter:

> 'Many factors are relevant, but in such a case as the present, particular importance may be attached to who may give orders as to how the work was to be done. If this power to control the method of performing the work is transferred from the general employer (M1) to the temporary employer (M2) then the latter may be liable. But, this is not so here.'

Viscount Simon:

> 'The permanent employer carries the burden of proving responsibility for the servant has shifted to the temporary employer ... I see the test as being - who had the authority to direct or delegate to the workman the manner in which the vehicle was driven? Here, in operating the crane the driver was using his own discretion which had been delegated to him by his regular employers. If he made a mistake in operating the crane, this was nothing to do with the hirers.'

Pao On v Law Yiu Long [1980] AC 614

See Chapter 4.

Ready Mixed Concrete (South East) Ltd v Minister of Pensions and National Insurance [1968] 2 WLR 775 High Court (MacKenna J)

Employee or independent contractor?

Facts

The plaintiff company devised a scheme whereby concrete was to be delivered to its customers ready-mixed. L entered into a contract with the company to deliver such concrete on a daily basis. L was to buy, run, maintain, repair, insure and drive his own lorry. He was paid by the company on a mileage plus bonus basis. He was subject to all the rules and regulations of the company which had a high degree of control over him and his work. Was L an employee or an independent contractor?

Held

He was an independent contractor as the provisions of his contract were inconsistent with its being a contract of service.

MacKenna J:

A contract of service exists if the following three conditions are fulfilled:

'(i) The servant agrees that in consideration of a wage or other remuneration he will provide his own work and skill in the performance of some service for his master. (ii) He agrees, expressly or impliedly, that in the performance of that service he will be subject to the other's control in a sufficient degree to make that other master. (iii) The other provisions of the contract are consistent with its being a contract of service.'

Rondel v Worsley [1969] 1 AC 191; [1967] 3 WLR 1666

See Chapter 1.

Rylands v Fletcher (1868) LR 3 HL 330 House of Lords (Lord Cairns LC and Lord Cranworth)

Escape of dangerous things

Facts

The plaintiff built a colliery on his land. One shaft was extended to join up with some old shafts which had been excavated under land adjacent to the plaintiff's. Using competent but, on this occasion, negligent independent contractors, the defendants constructed a reservoir on nearby land under which some of the old mine shafts were situated. When they filled the reservoir, the water entered the old shafts and, by that route, flooded the plaintiff's mine. The defendants themselves had not been negligent.

Held

The defendants were liable for the damage caused. Their Lordships approved the judgment of Blackburn J in the Court of Exchequer Chamber in which he said:

'The question therefore arises what is the obligation which the law casts upon a person who, like the defendants, lawfully brings onto his land something which though harmless while it remains there, will do mischief if it escapes ...

We think the true rule of law is that the person who for his own purposes brings onto his lands and collects and keeps there anything likely to do mischief if it escapes, must keep it in at his peril and if he does not do so, is prima facie liable for all the damage which is the natural consequence of its escape. He can excuse himself by showing that the escape was owing to the plaintiffs' default or, perhaps, that the escape was the consequence of vis major or Act of God but as nothing of this sort exists here, it is unnecessary to inquire what excuse would be sufficient.

The general rule as stated above, seems on principle just. The person whose grass or corn is eaten down by the escaping cattle of his neighbour or whose mine is flooded by water from his neighbour's reservoir or whose cellar is invaded by the filth of his neighbour's privy or whose habitat is made unhealthy by the fumes and noisome vapours of his neighbour's alkali works, is dominified without any fault of his own and it seems but reasonable and just that the neighbour who has brought something on his own property which was not naturally there, harmless to others so far as it is confined to his own property but which he knows will be mischievous if it gets on his neighbour's, should be obliged to make good the damage which ensues if he does not succeed in confining it to his own property.

... And upon authority this we think is established to be the law whether the things so brought be beasts or water or filth or stenches.'

Lord Cairns LC:

'... if the defendants not stopping at the natural use of their close (land) had desired to use it for any purpose which I may term non-natural use for the purpose of introducing into the close that which in its natural use was not in or upon it ... then it appears to me that that which the defendants were doing they were doing at their own peril.'

Sirros v Moore [1974] 3 WLR 459 Court of Appeal (Lord Denning MR, Buckley and Ormrod LJJ)

Judicial immunity

Facts

The plaintiff, a citizen of Turkey, was brought before a magistrate for breach of the Aliens Order 1953. He was fined £50 and the magistrate recommended that he be deported, adding that he should not be detained pending the Home Secretary's final decision as to deportation. The plaintiff's appeal to the Crown Court against the deportation recommendation was dismissed, but the circuit judge ordered police officers to detain the plaintiff and he was taken away in custody. The plaintiff sued the defendants, the circuit judge and the police officers, for damages for assault and false imprisonment.

Held

Although the plaintiff's detention had been unlawful (the appeal against the magistrate's order having merely been dismissed), the plaintiff had no cause of action against the circuit judge as he had acted judicially and under the honest (though mistaken) belief that his act was within his jurisdiction. No action lay against the police officers as they had acted at the judge's direction, not knowing it was wrong.

Lord Denning MR:

"Today we are concerned with judges of a new kind. The judges of the Crown Court. It is, by definition, a superior court of record; see section 4(1) of the 1971 Act. The judges of it should, in principle, have the same immunity as all other judges, high or low. The Crown Court is manned by judges of every rank. Judges of the High Court, circuit judges, recorders, justices of the peace, all sit there. No distinction can or should be drawn between them. Each one shares responsibility for the decisions given by the court. If the High Court judge is not liable to an action, it should be the same with the circuit judge, the recorder or the justice of the peace. No distinction can be taken on the seriousness of the case. Any one of them may sit on one day on a case of trifling importance, on the next on a case of the utmost gravity. No distinction can be taken as to the nature of the case. It may be a matter triable only on indictment, or it may be a man up for sentence, or an appeal from magistrates. If they are not liable in trials on indictment, they should not be liable on other matters. But, whatever it is, the immunity of the judges - and each of them - should rest on the same principle. Not liable for acts done by them in a judicial capacity. Only liable for acting in bad faith, knowing they have no jurisdiction to do it.

Smith v Leech Brain & Co Ltd [1962] 2 WLR 148 High Court (Lord Parker CJ)

Negligence - remoteness of damages

Facts

Due to the failure of the defendant employers to provide a safe system of working, the plaintiff's husband was burnt on the lip by a piece of molten metal. Soon after, the lip began to swell and cancer was diagnosed. Despite treatment, the plaintiff's husband died of the cancer some three years later. The evidence showed that the deceased had a pre-malignant condition, promoted into cancer by the burn.

Held

The plaintiff's claim against the defendants in respect of her husband's death succeeded.

Lord Parker CJ:

'The test is not whether these defendants could reasonably have foreseen that a burn would cause cancer and that Mr Smith would die. The question is whether these defendants could reasonably foresee the type of injury which he suffered, namely, the burn. What, in the particular case, is the amount of damage which he suffers as a result of that burn, depends on the characteristics and constitution of the victim.'

Sturges v Bridgman (1879) 11 Ch D 852 Court of Appeal (Thesiger, James and Baggallay LJJ)

Nuisance - doctor's consulting room

Facts

The plaintiff was a doctor who bought premises in Wimpole Street. The defendant had a confectionery business in Wigmore Street, which runs at right angles to Wimpole Street. The defendant's kitchen abutted part of the plaintiff's garden. In the kitchen, against the abutting wall, the defendant had two mortars for pounding loaf sugar and meat; he had used them there for more than 20 years. Some eight years after he moved in, the plaintiff built a consulting room on the abutting wall. He alleged that the noise from the mortars then became a nuisance to him and he sought an injunction.

Held

The injunction would be granted. The defendant was not protected by prescription as until the consulting room was built there was no actionable nuisance.

Thesiger LJ:

'Whether anything is a nuisance or not is a question to be determined not merely by an abstract consideration of the thing itself, but with reference to its circumstances; what would be a nuisance in Belgrave Square would not necessarily be so in Bermondsey or where a locality is devoted to a particular trade or manufacture carried on by the traders in a particular or established manner not constituting a public nuisance. Judges and juries would be justified in finding and may be trusted to find, that the trade or manufacture so carried on in that locality is not a private or actionable wrong ... It would be on the one hand in a very high degree unreasonable and undesirable that there should be a right of action for acts which are not (in the present condition of the adjoining land) and perhaps never will be any inconvenience or annoyance and it would be on the other hand in an equal degree unjust that the use and value of the adjoining land should for all time and in all circumstances be diminished by reason of the continuance of acts incapable of physical interruption and which the law gives no power to prevent.'

Tarry v Ashton (1876) 1 QBD 314 High Court (Blackburn, Quain and Lush JJ)

Nuisance - negligent independent contractor

Facts

The defendant moved into a house which had a heavy lamp projecting from the front wall. After moving in, the defendant employed an experienced gas fitter, an independent contractor, to mend the lamp. Some months later, the lamp fell on and injured the plaintiff as she was walking along the pavement.

Held

The defendant was liable for the plaintiff's injuries.

Lush J:

'The question is what is the duty of a person in the position of the defendant? Is it his duty to maintain his premises in good repair, or only to employ a competent person in the work of maintaining them? I think the mere statement of the case suggests its answer. A person who keeps a lamp of this kind puts the public in peril. He cannot get rid of his duty to put the public out of peril by employing another person to take the necessary steps for doing so.'

Tolley v J S Fry and Sons Ltd [1931] AC 333 House of Lords (Lords Hailsham, Dunedin, Buckmaster, Blanesburgh and Tomlin)

Libel - defamatory meaning

Facts

The plaintiff was a well-known amateur golfer, the defendants manufacturers of chocolate. In June 1928, the defendants published in the Daily Sketch and Daily Mail a caricature of the plaintiff which showed him in golfing gear having just completed a drive with a packet of the defendants' chocolate protruding from his pocket. His caddie, too, held a packet of the defendants' chocolate and below there was a limerick:

'My word how it flies ... like a Frys ... etc.'

The plaintiff alleged there was a defamatory innuendo that the plaintiff had agreed to pose for an advertisement for reward, that he had prostituted his reputation as an amateur golfer and was guilty of conduct unworthy of amateur status.

Held (Lord Blanesburgh dissenting)

Although the words were not libellous, the imputation from them was and the plaintiff was entitled to succeed.

Twine v Bean's Express Ltd (1946) 175 LT 131 Court of Appeal (Lord Greene MR, Morton and Tucker LJJ)

Vicarious liability - unauthorised passenger

Facts

The plaintiff's husband was killed when the van in which he was being carried was involved in an accident due to the negligence of the driver, the defendants' servant.

The deceased and the driver knew that the giving of lifts to unauthorised persons was forbidden.

Held

The plaintiff's claim would fail as the driver was acting outside the scope of his employment.

Lord Greene MR:

'The deceased had no right to be in the van and the driver had no right to give him a lift; the deceased was therefore a trespasser and was owed no duty of care by the employers of the driver ... The driver, in giving a lift to the deceased, was clearly acting outside the scope of his employment. He had no right whatsoever to do such a thing and in this respect, he was on a frolic of his own.'

Universe Tankships Inc of Monrovia v International Transport Workers' Federation [1982] 2 WLR 803 House of Lords (Lords Diplock, Cross of Chelsea, Russell of Killowen, Scarman and Brandon of Oakbrook)

Trade dispute - duress

Facts

An international federation of trade unions had a policy of blacking vessels sailing under flags of convenience unless their owners complied with certain demands. Faced with this threat, the vessel owners in question made a payment, as required, on behalf of crew members to a welfare fund established under the federation's auspices. After their vessel had been allowed to sail the owners sought the recovery of this money on the ground, inter alia, that it had been exacted by subjecting them to economic duress. The federation conceded that the money had been so exacted.

Held

The contribution to the welfare fund was recoverable.

Lord Diplock:

'The use of economic duress to induce another person to part with property or money is not a tort per se; the form that the duress takes may, or may not, be tortious. The remedy to which economic duress gives rise is not an action for damages but an action for restitution of property or money exacted under such duress and the avoidance of any contract that had been induced by it; but where the particular form taken by the economic duress used is itself a tort, the restitutional remedy for money had and received by the defendant to the plaintiff's use is one which the plaintiff is entitled to pursue as an alternative remedy to an action for damage in tort.'

See also Chapter 4.

Wheat v E Lacon & Co Ltd [1966] 2 WLR 581 House of Lords (Viscount Dilhorne, Lords Denning, Morris of Borth-y-Gest, Pearce and Pearson)

Negligence - occupation or control

Facts

The respondent brewery company owned a public house, the first floor of which was the living quarters of the resident manager and his wife, who occasionally took in paying guests. The appellant and her husband took a room there. At about 9.00 pm one evening the appellant's husband slipped and fell down the stairs from the first floor and was killed. The cause of the accident was found to be (a) that the handrail did not go right to the bottom of the stairs, and (b) the light at the top of the stairs was missing. The appellant sued the respondents, alleging they were in breach of their common duty of care under the Occupiers' Liability Act 1957.

Held

The respondents, together with the manager and his wife, were occupiers of the premises and owed a duty of care to all lawful visitors. However, the facts disclosed no breach of duty so the appeal was dismissed.

Lord Denning:

'... wherever a person has a sufficient degree of control over premises that he ought to realise that any failure to use care of his part may result in injury to a person coming lawfully there, then he is an "occupier" and the persons coming there are his "visitors"; and the "occupier" is under a duty to the "visitor" to use reasonable care. In order to be an occupier, it is not necessary for a person to have entire control over the premises. He need not have exclusive occupation. Suffice it that he has some degree of control. He may share control with others. Two or more may be occupiers. And, whenever this happens, each is under a duty to use care towards persons coming lawfully on the premises, dependent on his degree of control ... any degree of control over the state of the premises may be enough (to make a person an occupier).'

Wilkinson v Downton [1897] 2 QB 57 High Court (Wright J)

Damages - nervous disorders

Facts

The defendant, as a practical joke, falsely told the plaintiff that the plaintiff's husband had been smashed up in an accident and was lying at a pub with both legs broken and that she was to take a car and fetch him home. As a result, the plaintiff suffered severe nervous disorders, she vomited and needed medical treatment.

Held

The plaintiff could recover damages for her injuries.

Wright J:

'This claim cannot succeed on the basis of fraud, but it can succeed on the ground that the defendant has wilfully done an act calculated to cause physical harm to the plaintiff - that is to infringe her legal right to personal safety and has, in fact, thereby caused physical harm to her ... Such an intention can be imputed on the facts. The injuries were not too remote. Suppose that a person is in a precarious and dangerous condition and another person tells him that his physician has said he has but a day to live ... if a serious aggravation of illness ensued, damages might be recovered.'

4 CONTRACT AND CONSUMER LAW

Adams v Lindsell (1818) 1 B & Ald 681 King's Bench (Lord Ellenborough)

Offer and acceptance - acceptance by post

Facts

On 2 September, the defendants wrote to the plaintiffs, offering a quantity of wool on certain conditions and requiring an answer 'in course of post'. The defendants misdirected the letter, which did not arrive until 5 September. The plaintiffs immediately sent a letter of acceptance which was delivered on 9 September. But on 8 September, a day after they could have expected to receive a reply if the initial letter had been properly addressed, the defendants had sold the wool to third parties.

Held

As soon as the letter of acceptance was posted on 5 September, it was effective, and a valid contract was concluded.

American Cyanamid Co v Ethicon Ltd [1975] AC 396 House of Lords (Viscount Dilhorne, Lords Diplock, Cross, Salmon and Edmund-Davies)

Interlocutory injunctions - principle governing grant

Facts

The plaintiffs believed that the defendants were about to infringe their patent relating to surgical sutures and they sought an interlocutory injunction.

Held

The injunction would be granted.

See also Chapter 1.

Anglia Television Ltd v Reed [1972] 1 QB 60 Court of Appeal (Lord Denning MR, Phillimore and Megaw LJJ)

Breach of contract - measure of damages

Facts

The plaintiffs were minded in 1968 to make a film of a play for television entitled 'The Man in the Wood' and they made many arrangements in advance. They arranged for a place where the play was to be filmed. They employed a director, a designer and a stage manager and so forth. They involved themselves in much expense. All this was done before they got the leading man. They required a strong actor capable of holding the play together. He was to be on the scene the whole time. They eventually found the man, the defendant, an American who has a very high reputation as an actor. By telephone conversation on 30 August 1968, it was agreed by Mr Reed, through his agent, that he would come to England and be available between 9 September and 11 October 1968 to rehearse and play in this film. He was to get a performance fee of £1,050, living expenses of £100 a week, his first class fares to and from the United States and so forth. It was all subject to the permit of the Ministry of Labour for him to come here. That was duly given on 2 September 1968 so the contract was concluded. But unfortunately, there was some muddle with the bookings: the defendant's agents had already booked him in America for some other play. So, on 3 September 1968 the agent said that the defendant would not come to England to perform in this play. He repudiated his contract. The plaintiffs tried hard to find a substitute but could not do so. So on 11 September they accepted his repudiation. They abandoned the proposed film and then sued Mr Reed for damages. He did not dispute his liability, but a question arose as to the damages, the plaintiffs claiming for the wasted expenditure - the director's fees, the designer's fees, the stage manager's and assistant manager's fees, and so on.

Held

They were entitled to succeed.

Lord Denning MR:

'It seems to me that a plaintiff in such a case as this has an election: he can either claim for loss of profits or for his wasted expenditure. But he must elect between them. He cannot claim both. If he has not suffered any loss of profits - or if he cannot prove what his profits would have been - he can claim in the alternative the expenditure which has been thrown away, that is, wasted by reason of the breach.

If the plaintiff claims the wasted expenditure, he is not limited to the expenditure incurred after the contract was concluded. He can claim also the expenditure incurred before the contract, provided that it was such as would reasonably be in the contemplation of the parties as likely to be wasted if the contract was broken. Applying that principle here, it is plain that when Mr Reed entered into his contract, he must have known perfectly well that much expenditure had already been incurred on director's fee and the like. He must have contemplated - or, at any rate, it is reasonably to be imputed to him - that if he broke his contract, all that expenditure would be wasted, whether or not it was incurred before or after the contract. He must pay damages for all the expenditure so wasted and thrown away.

It is true that if the defendant had never entered into the contract, he would not be liable and the expenditure would have been incurred by the plaintiff without redress; but the defendant, having made his contract and broken it, it does not lie in his mouth to say he is not liable when it was because of his breach that the expenditure has been wasted.'

Ashbury Railway Carriage & Iron Co v Riche (1875) LR 7 HL 653 House of Lords (Lord Cairns LC, Lords Chelmsford, Hatherley, O'Hagan and Selborne)

Company - contract ultra vires

Facts

The company's objects set out in its Memorandum of Association enabled it to manufacture, sell and hire railway plant, fittings and rolling stock. The company contracted to finance the construction of a railway, but repudiated and was sued.

Held

The contract was ultra vires and the company was not liable thereon because it was outside the scope of the objects clause.

Lord Cairns LC:

'... the question is as to the competency and power of the company to make the contract. Now I am clearly of the opinion that this contract was entirely, as I have said, beyond the objects of the memorandum of the association. If so, it was thereby placed beyond the powers of the company to make the contract. If so, it is not a question whether the contract ever was ratified or was not ratified. It was a contract void at its beginning, it was void because the company could not make the contract.'

Balfour v Balfour [1919] 2 KB 571 Court of Appeal (Warrington, Duke and Atkin LJJ)

Agreement - no intention that it be enforceable

Facts

After their marriage, the parties went to Ceylon where the husband was director of immigration. Fifteen years later they came home on leave. On medical advice, it was decided that the wife should remain in England, but she alleged that, as the husband was about to sail back to Ceylon, he had entered into an oral contract to make her an allowance of £30 a month until she rejoined him in Ceylon. At that time they had not agreed to live apart, although they subsequently did so when differences arose. The wife sought to recover money allegedly due to her under the oral agreement.

Held

Her action would fail as there was no contract in a legal sense.

Beale v Taylor [1967] 1 WLR 1193 Court of Appeal (Sellers and Danckwerts LJJ and Baker J)

Sale by description - motor car

Facts

The defendant advertised a car for sale as a 'Herald convertible, white, 1961, twin carbs'. The plaintiff answered the advertisement, went to the defendant's home, and having inspected the car there, bought it. Neither realised at the time that the rear half of the car was from a 1961 Herald convertible, that the front half was from an earlier model and that the two halves had been welded together. No one could see from an ordinary examination of the car that it was anything other than what the defendant had advertised it to be. On discovering the true position, the plaintiff brought an action against the defendant for damages under s13 of the Sale of Goods Act 1893 for breach of condition. The defendant contended that the plaintiff had seen the car before buying it and had then bought it on his own assessment of its value.

Held

The plaintiff was entitled to succeed.

Seller LJ:

'The question in this case is whether this was a sale by description or whether, as the seller contends, this was a sale of a particular thing seen by the buyer and bought by him purely on his own assessment of the value of the thing to him. We were referred to a passage in the speech of Lord Wright in *Grant v Australian Knitting Mills Ltd*, which I think is apt as far as this case is concerned. Lord Wright said:

"It may also be pointed out that there is a sale by description even though the buyer is buying something displayed before him on the counter, a thing is sold by description, though it is specific, so long as it is sold not merely as the specific thing but as a thing corresponding to a description, eg woollen undergarments, a hot water bottle, a second-hand reaping machine, to select a few obvious illustrations"

- and, I might add, a second-hand motor car. I think that, on the facts of this case, the buyer, when he came along to see this car, was coming along to see a car as advertised, that is, a car described as a "Herald convertible, white, 1961". When he came along he saw what ostensibly was a Herald convertible, white, 1961, because the evidence shows that the "1200" which was exhibited on the rear of this motor car is the first model of the "1200" which came out in 1961; it was on that basis that he was making the offer and in the belief that the seller was advancing his car as that which his advertisement indicated.'

Beswick v Beswick [1967] AC 58 House of Lords (Lords Reid, Hodson, Guest, Pearce and Upjohn)

Contract - enforcement by stranger to it

Facts

Peter Beswick was a coal merchant. In 1962 he contracted with John Beswick, his nephew, to sell the business in consideration of: (1) that for the rest of Peter's life, John would pay him £6.10s per week; (2) that if Peter's wife survived him, John would pay her £5 a week. John took over the business and paid the agreed sum to Peter until he died in November 1963. He made one payment of £5 to Peter's widow and then ceased payments. The widow commenced proceedings, claiming arrears and specific performance and brought the action both as administratrix of the deceased husband's estate and in her own capacity.

Held

The widow was entitled, as administratrix, to an order for specific performance, but the effect of ss56(1) and 205(1)(xx) of the Law of property Act 1925 was not to confer upon a third party any right to sue upon a contract.

Bridge v Campbell Discount Co Ltd [1962] AC 600 House of Lords (Viscount Simonds, Lords Morton of Henryton, Radcliffe, Denning and Devlin)

Hire-purchase agreement - penalty clause?

Facts

The appellant hirer entered into a hire-purchase agreement with the respondents in respect of a used car. Under the agreement, it could be terminated by the hirer, but he was then obliged forthwith to deliver up the vehicle, pay any arrears with interest 'and by way of agreed compensation for the depreciation of the vehicle such further sum as may be necessary to make the rentals paid and payable hereunder equal to two-thirds of the hire-purchase price.' Having paid the initial payment and the first instalment, the appellant terminated the agreement and returned the car. The respondents sued to recover two-thirds of the price, less the payments made.

Held

Their claim would fail as the relevant clause made provision for a penalty.

Lord Morton of Henryton:

'... the appellant has clearly committed a breach of the hire-purchase agreement by failing to pay the subsequent instalments, and it becomes necessary to consider whether the payment stipulated [in] the agreement was a penalty or liquidated damages.

"The essence of a penalty is a payment of money stipulated as in terrorem of the offending party; the essence of liquidated damages is a genuine covenanted pre-estimate of damage."

See per Lord Dunedin in *Dunlop Pneumatic Tyre Co Ltd* v *New Garage & Motor Co Ltd*. I find it impossible to regard the sum stipulated ... as a genuine pre-estimate of the loss which would be suffered by the respondents in the events specified in the same clause. One reason will suffice, though others might be given. This was a second-hand car when the appellant took it over on hire-purchase. The depreciation in its value would naturally become greater the longer it remained in the appellant's hands. Yet the sum to be paid ... is largest when, as in the present case, the car is returned after it has been in the hirer's possession for a very short time, and gets progressively smaller as time goes on. This could not possibly be the result of a genuine pre-estimate of the loss. Further, in my view, the provisions ... were "stipulated as in terrorem" of the appellant. As counsel for the appellant put it: "They are intended to secure that the hirer will not determine the agreement until at least two-thirds of the price has been paid." The result is that the appellant is entitled to relief ...'

Brinkibon Ltd v Stahag Stahl und Stahlwarenhandelsgesellschaft mbH [1983] 2 AC 34 House of Lords (Lords Wilberforce, Fraser of Tullybelton, Russell of Killowen, Bridge of Harwich and Brandon of Oakbrook)

Offer and acceptance - acceptance by telex

Facts

Following negotiations relating to steel bars to be delivered from Egypt, an English company accepted, by telex sent from London to Vienna, the terms of sale offered by an Austrian company.

Held

The contract had been made in Austria and it followed that the English court did not have jurisdiction in relation to it.

Lord Wilberforce:

'... with a general rule covering instantaneous communication inter praesentes, or at a distance, with an exception applying to non-instantaneous communication at a distance, how should communications by telex be categorised? In *Entores Ltd* v *Miles Far East Corp* the Court of Appeal classified them with instantaneous communications. Their ruling ... appears not to have caused either adverse comment, or any difficulty to businessmen. I would accept it as a general rule. Where the condition of simultaneity is met, and where it appears to be within the mutual intention of the parties that contractual exchanges should take place in this way, I think it a sound rule, but not necessarily a universal rule.

Since 1955 the use of telex communication has been greatly expanded, and there are many variants on it. The senders and recipients may not be the principals to the contemplated contract. They may be servants or agents with limited authority. The message may not reach, or be intended to reach, the designated recipient immediately: messages may be sent out of office hours, or at night, with the intention, or on the assumption, that they will be read at a later time. There may be some error or default at the recipient's end which prevents receipt at the time contemplated and believed in by the sender. The message may have been sent and/or received through machines operated by third persons. And many other variations may occur. No universal rule can cover all such cases; they must be resolved by reference to the intentions of the parties, by sound business practice and in some cases by a judgment where the risks should lie ...'

Brogden v Metropolitan Rail Co (1877) 2 App Cas 666 House of Lords (Lord Cairns LC, Lords Hatherley, Selborne, Blackburn and Gordon)

Contract - creation by conduct

Facts

Brogden had for years supplied the railway company with coal without a formal agreement. Wishing to regularise the situation, the company sent a draft form of agreement to Brodgen, who inserted the name of an arbitrator in a space left blank for this purpose, signed it and returned it marked 'approved'. The company's agent put it in his desk and there it lay for two years with nothing further being done to complete its execution. Both parties acted thereafter on the strength of its terms, supplying and paying for coal in accordance with the terms of the draft agreement. After two years, a dispute arose and Brogden denied that any binding contract existed.

Held

A contract had been created by conduct and it came into existence either when the company ordered its first load of coal upon the terms of the draft, or at least when Brogden supplied it.

Butler Machine Tool Co Ltd v Ex-Cell-O Corporation (England) Ltd [1979] 1 WLR 401 Court of Appeal (Lord Denning MR, Lawton and Bridge LJJ)

Offer and acceptance - counter - offer - battle of forms

Facts

In response to the appellants' enquiry, the respondents offered to sell them a machine tool, delivery in ten months' time, and the offer was stated to be subject to certain terms and conditions which 'shall prevail over any terms and conditions in the buyer's order'. The respondents placed an order, subject to terms and conditions which were materially different to those of the appellants. At the foot of the respondents' form of order was a tear-off acknowledgment stating 'We accept your order on the terms and conditions stated thereon': this the appellants signed and returned accompanied by a letter stating that the order was being entered in accordance with the appellants' quotation. The original offer or quotation contained a price variation clause; the respondents' terms and conditions did not.

Held

There was a fixed price contract as the appellants had accepted what was, in effect, the respondents' counter-offer.

Byrne & Co v Leon van Tienhoven & Co (1880) 5 CPD 344 Court of Common Pleas (Lindley J)

Offer by post - revocation

Facts

On 1 October, the defendants in Cardiff posted a letter to the plaintiffs in New York, offering to sell them 1,000 boxes of tin plates. On 8 October, the defendants posted a letter revoking the offer. On 11 October, the plaintiffs telegraphed their acceptance. On 15 October, the plaintiffs confirmed their acceptance by letter. On 20 October, the defendants' letter of revocation reached the plaintiffs.

Held

There was a contract as the revocation of the offer was inoperative until it was actually received on 20 October.

Lindley J:

> '... the writer of the offer has expressly or impliedly assented to treat an answer to him by a letter duly posted as a sufficient acceptance or notification to himself, or, in other words, he has made the Post Office his agent to receive the acceptance and notification of it. But this principle appears to me to be inapplicable to the case of a withdrawal of an offer ... If the defendant's contentions were to prevail, no person who had received an offer by post and had accepted it, would know his position until he had waited such a time as to be quite sure that a letter withdrawing the offer had not been posted before his acceptance of it.'

Carlill v Carbolic Smoke Ball Co [1893] 1 QB 256 Court of Appeal (Lindley, Bowen and A L Smith LJJ)

Offer to the world - acceptance

Facts

The defendants issued a newspaper advertisement in which they said they would pay £100 to any person who contracted influenza after using one of their smoke balls in a specified manner for a specific period. They also stated that they had deposited £1,000 with a named bank, to show their sincerity in the matter.

The plaintiff, believing the accuracy of the advertisement, purchased one of the balls and used it as directed - but she caught 'flu nevertheless! She sued to recover the £100.

Held

She was entitled to succeed.

Casey's Patents, Re, Stewart v Casey [1892] 1 Ch 104 Court of Appeal (Lindley, Bowen and Fry LJJ)

Consideration - past service

Facts

Stewart and Charlton, joint owners of certain patent rights, wrote to the defendant, Casey, saying that '... in consideration of your services as the practical manager in working both our patents ... we hereby agree to give you one third share of the patents ...' The patents were subsequently transferred to Casey. The plaintiffs now claimed their return.

Held

The action would be dismissed.

Bowen LJ:

> 'Even if it were true ... that a past service cannot support a future promise, you must look at the document and see if the promise cannot receive a proper effect in some other way. Now, the fact of a past service raises an implication that at the time it was rendered it was to be paid for and, if it was a service that was to be paid for, when you get in the subsequent document a promise to pay, that promise may be treated either as an admission which evidences, or as a positive bargain which fixes the amount of that reasonable remuneration on the faith of which the service was originally rendered.'

Central London Property Trust Ltd v High Trees House Ltd [1947] KB 130 High Court (Denning J)

Promise without consideration - estoppel

Facts

By a lease of 1937, the plaintiffs leased a block of flats to the defendants for 99 years at a rent of £2,500 pa. With the advent of war and many vacancies in the flats, the plaintiffs agreed in 1940 to reduce the rent by 50 per cent. No time limit was set for the reduction. By 1945 the flats were full again. The plaintiff company thereupon wrote to the defendants, asking for the full amount of rent plus arrears. Subsequently, the present action was instituted to test the legal position. The plaintiffs claimed the full rent for the last two quarters of 1945. The defendants pleaded, inter alia, that the agreement of 1940 related to the whole term of the lease; or, alternatively, that by failing to demand rent in excess of £1,250 before September 1945, the plaintiffs had waived their rights in respect of any rent in excess of that amount which had accrued before that date.

Held

The plaintiffs' claim would succeed although, as regards the earlier period, the promise to reduce the rent was binding even though it had been given without consideration.

Denning J:

> 'I find that the conditions prevailing at the time when the reduction in rent was made, had completely passed away by the early months of 1945. I am satisfied that the promise was understood by all parties only to apply under the conditions prevailing at the time when it was made, namely, when the

flats were only partially let, and that it did not extend any further than that. When the flats became fully let, early in 1945, the reduction ceased to apply.

In those circumstances, under the law as I hold it, it seems to me that rent is payable at the full rate for the quarters ending 29 September and 25 December 1945.

If the case had been one of estoppel, it might be said that in any event the estoppel would cease when the conditions to which the representation applied came to an end, or it also might be said that it would only come to an end on notice. In either case it is only a way of ascertaining what is the scope of the representation. I prefer to apply the principle that a promise intended to be binding, intended to be acted on and in fact acted on, is binding so far as its terms properly apply. Here it was binding as covering the period down to the early part of 1945, and as from that time full rent is payable.'

Clea Shipping Corporation v Bulk Oil International Ltd, The Alaskan Trader [1984] 1 All ER 129 High Court (Lloyd J)

Repudiation of contract - victim's choices

Facts

C chartered a ship to B. After a year (the charter was for two years), the ship broke down and was put in for repairs. B informed C that it no longer wanted the ship, but C carried out the repairs and, on their completion, offered the ship as ready once again; again B said it was not wanted. C took no steps to find an alternative charterer and kept the ship fully crewed. Was C entitled to continue performance of the contract, or should it have repudiated it and sued for damages?

Held

The court would not interfere with the arbitrator's finding that C should have accepted the repudiation made on completion of the repairs and could not recover the cost of hire under the charter party; instead C had to sue for breach of contract.

Clements v London and North Western Railway Co [1894] 2 QB 482 (Lord Esher, Kay and A L Smith LJJ)

Minor - insurance scheme

Facts

An infant, on entering the service of the defendant railway company, agreed to join the company's insurance scheme, thereby giving up any claim for personal injury he may have had under the relevant statute, the Employers' Liability Act 1880. The scheme was, in some ways, more favourable than his entitlements under the Act, but in other ways less beneficial.

Held

As the contract was, on the whole, beneficial to the infant, he was bound by it.

Collins v Godefroy (1831) 1 B & AD 950 King's Bench (Lord Tenterden CJ)

Consideration - promisee subpoenaed

Facts

C had been subpoenaed by G to attend as a witness in an action. C subsequently brought an action against G, claiming a guinea a day as his fee for attendance. Assuming that G had expressly promised to pay the sum claimed as compensation for loss of time, was there any consideration for the promise?

Held

There was not.

Lord Tenterden CJ:

> 'If it be a duty imposed by law upon a party regularly subpoenaed to attend from time to time to give his evidence, then a promise to give him any remuneration for loss of time incurred in such attendance is a promise without consideration.'

Cutter v Powell (1795) 6 Term Rep 320 Court of King's Bench (Lord Kenyon CJ, Ashhurst, Grose and Lawrence JJ)

Incomplete performance

Facts

The defendant, master of the Governor Parry, contracted to pay a seaman 30 guineas 'provided he proceeds, continues, and does his duty as second mate in the said ship from hence [Kingston, Jamaica] to the port of Liverpool'. The seaman died in the course of the voyage and his administratrix sued for work and labour done.

Held

Her action could not succeed.

Ashhurst J:

> 'This is a written contract, and it speaks for itself. As it is entire and, as the defendant's promise depends on a condition precedent to be performed by the other party, the condition must be performed before the other party is entitled to receive anything under it. It has been argued, however, that the plaintiff may now recover on a quantum meruit, but she has no right to desert the agreement for whenever there is an express contract the parties must be guided by it, and one party cannot relinquish or abide by it as it may suit his advantage. Here the intestate was by the terms of his contract to perform a given duty before he could call on the defendant to pay him anything; it was a condition precedent, without performing which the defendant is not liable. That seems to me to conclude the question. The intestate did not perform the contract on his part; he was not indeed to blame for not doing it; but still as this was a condition precedent, and as he did not perform it, his representative is not entitled to recover.'

D & C Builders Ltd v Rees [1966] 2 WLR 288 Court of Appeal (Lord Denning MR, Danckwerts and Winn LJJ)

Debt - acceptance of smaller sum

Facts

The plaintiffs (D & C Builders) were a small firm who did work for the defendant, for which he owed them £482. After the amount had been outstanding for some time, the defendant's wife, acting for the defendant and knowing that the plaintiffs were in financial difficulties, offered them £300 in settlement. She said the plaintiffs could have £300 or nothing and rejected an offer to find the disputed £182 over a further twelve months. The plaintiffs reluctantly agreed, since without the £300 their firm would have gone bankrupt. The plaintiffs then sued for the balance.

Held

The plaintiffs' action was not barred: there had been no true accord and there was no equitable ground for rejecting their claim.

Lord Denning MR:

'... it is a daily occurrence that a merchant or tradesman, who is owed a sum of money, is asked to take less. The debtor says he is in difficulties. ... The creditor ... accepts the proffered sum and forgives him the rest of the debt. The question arises: is the settlement binding on the creditor? The answer is that, in point of law, the creditor is not bound by the settlement. He can, the next day, sue the debtor for the balance and get judgment ...

This doctrine of the common law has come under heavy fire ... But a remedy has been found. The harshness of the common law has been relieved. Equity has stretched out a merciful hand to help the debtor. The courts have invoked the broad principle stated by Lord Cairns LC in *Hughes* v *Metropolitan Rail Co* ... This principle has been applied to cases where a creditor agrees to accept a lesser sum in discharge of a greater ... In applying this principle, however, he must note the qualification. The creditor is barred from his legal rights only when it would be *inequitable* for him to insist on them. Where there has been a *true accord* under which the creditor voluntarily agrees to accept a lesser sum in satisfaction and the debtor *acts on* that accordance by paying the lesser sum and the creditor accepts it, then it is inequitable for the creditor afterwards to insist on the balance. But he is not bound unless there has been truly an accord between them.

In the present case, on the facts as found by the judge, it seems to me that there was no true accord. The debtor's wife held the creditor to ransom. The creditor was in need of money to meet his own commitments, and she knew it. When the creditor asked for payment of the £480 due to him, she said to him in effect: "We cannot pay you the £480. But we will pay you £300 if you will accept it in settlement. If you do not accept it on those terms, you will get nothing. £300 is better than nothing." She had no right to say any such thing. She could properly have said: "We cannot pay you more than £300. Please accept it on account." But she had no right to insist on his taking it in settlement. When she said: "We will pay you nothing unless you accept £300 in settlement," she was putting undue pressure on the creditor. She was making a threat to break the contract (by paying nothing) and she was doing it so as to compel the creditor to do what he was unwilling to do (to accept £300 in settlement): and she succeeded. He complied with her demand. That was ... a case of intimidation ... In these circumstances there was no true accord so as to found a defence of accord and satisfaction ... There is also no equity in the defendant to warrant any departure from the due course of law. No person can insist on a settlement procured by intimidation.'

Dakin (H) & Co Ltd v Lee [1916] 1 KB 566 Court of Appeal (Lord Cozens-Hardy MR, Warrington and Pickford LJJ)

Performance - defective work

Facts

The plaintiff builders contracted to execute certain repairs to the defendant's premises. They carried out a substantial part of the work, but failed to perform it exactly in three unimportant respects.

Held

The plaintiffs were entitled to recover the contract price less a reduction for the defective work.

Lord Cozens-Hardy MR:

'Take a contract for a lump sum to decorate a house; the contract provides that there shall be three coats of oil paint, but in one of the rooms only two coats of paint are put on. Can anyone seriously say that under these circumstances the building owner could go and occupy the house and take the benefit of all the decorations which had been done in the other rooms without paying a penny for all the work done by the builder, just because only two coats of paint had been put on in one room where there ought to have been three?'

Daulia Ltd v Four Millbank Nominees Ltd [1978] 2 WLR 621 Court of Appeal (Buckley, Orr and Goff LJJ)

Oral offer to enter into written contract

Facts

The defendants wanted to sell certain properties and the plaintiffs were anxious to buy them. On 21 December the parties agreed terms and further agreed to exchange contracts the next day. When the plaintiffs attended the defendants' offices on 22 December to exchange the contracts, the defendants, who had in the meantime found another purchaser willing to pay a higher price, refused to complete the sale. The plaintiffs sued for breach of contract alleging that on 21 December, an agent of the defendants had promised them that if they attended at the defendants' offices the next morning and gave the defendants a signed and engrossed copy of the contract, together with a banker's draft for the deposit, the defendants would enter into a written contract with them for the sale of the properties.

Held

Assuming the facts to be as alleged, since the contract was for disposition of an interest in land and it was not in writing, it fell foul of s40(1) Law of Property Act 1925 and, accordingly, the plaintiffs' claim for damages for breach of contract would be struck out.

Goff LJ:

> 'Whilst I think the true view of a unilateral contract must, in general, be that the offeror is entitled to require full performance of the condition which he has imposed and, short of that, he is not bound; that must be subject to one important qualification, which stems from the fact that there must be an implied obligation on the part of the offeror not to prevent the condition becoming satisfied, which obligation, it seems to me, must arise as soon as the offeree starts to perform. Until then, the offeror can revoke the whole thing, but once the offeree has embarked on performance, it is too late for the offeror to revoke his offer.'

Davis Contractors Ltd v Fareham Urban District Council [1956] AC 696 House of Lords (Viscount Simonds, Lords Morton of Henryton, Reid, Radcliffe and Somervell of Harrow)

Building contract - completion delayed

Facts

The contractors agreed to build houses for the defendant local authority over a period of eight months for a fixed price. Mainly due to labour shortages, the building took almost two years and cost the contractors more than the agreed price. They commenced proceedings, claiming the contract was frustrated and they were entitled to quantum meruit for the work done.

Held

The contract was not frustrated.

Lord Reid:

> 'Frustration has often been said to depend on adding a term to the contract by implication ... I find great difficulty in accepting this as the correct approach ...
>
> It appears to me that frustration depends, at least in most cases, not on adding any implied term, but on the true construction of the terms which are in the contract, read in light of the nature of the contract and of the relevant surrounding circumstances when the contract was made ... The question is whether the contract which they make is, on its true construction, wide enough to apply to the new situation, if it is not, then it is at an end.

In my view, the proper approach to this case is to take ... all facts which throw light on the nature of the contract, or which can properly be held to be intrinsic evidence relevant to assist in its construction and then, as a matter of law, to construe the contract and to determine whether the ultimate situation ... is or is not within the scope of the contract so construed.

De Francesco v Barnum (1890) 45 Ch D 430 High Court (Fry LJ)

Minor - dancing apprenticeship

Facts

By a deed a minor was apprenticed to the plaintiff for seven years to be instructed in stage dancing. Under the deed, inter alia, the minor would not marry during that time and her services would be entirely at the plaintiff's disposal: no provision was made for remuneration, except during an engagement, or for clothes, lodging or food, except when working abroad. The deed also provided that the plaintiff could terminate the apprenticeship at any time. The minor accepted an engagement in breach of the deed and the plaintiff sought, inter alia, an injunction.

Held

His action would fail.

Fry LJ:

'I approach this subject with the observation that it appears to me the question is: Is the contract for the benefit of the infant? Not, Is any one particular stipulation for the benefit of the infant? Because it is obvious that the contract of apprenticeship or the contract of labour must, like any other contract, contain some stipulations for the benefit of the one contracting party, and some for the benefit of the other. It is not because you can lay your hand on a particular stipulation which you may say is against the infant's benefit that therefore the whole contract is not for the benefit of the infant. The court must look at the whole contract, having regard to the circumstances of the case, and determine subject to any principles of law which may be ascertained by the cases, whether the contract is or is not beneficial. That appears to me to be in substance a question of fact ...'

Dickinson v Dodds (1876) 2 Ch D 463 Court of Appeal (James, Mellish and Baggallay LJJ)

Offer - withdrawal

Facts

On 10 June, the defendant delivered to the plaintiff a written offer to sell a certain house ' to be left open until Friday 12 June, 9.00 am'. On Thursday 11 June, the defendant sold the house to a third party, Allan. That evening, the plaintiff was told of the sale by a fourth man. Before 9.00 am on 12 June, the plaintiff handed to the defendant a formal letter of acceptance.

Held

The defendant had validly withdrawn his offer and the plaintiff's purported acceptance was too late.

James LJ:

'It appears to me that there is neither principle nor authority for the proposition that there must be an express and actual withdrawal of the offer, or what is called a retractation. It must, to constitute a contract, appear that the two minds were as one, at the same moment of time, that is, that there was an offer continuing up to the time of the acceptance. If there was not such a continuing offer, then the acceptance comes to nothing. Of course it may well be that the one man is bound in some way or other to let the other man know that his mind with regard to the offer has been changed; but in this case, beyond all question, the plaintiff knew that Dodds was no longer minded to sell the property to him as plainly and clearly as if Dodds had told him in so many words, "I withdraw the offer." This is evident from the plaintiff's own statements in the bill ... It is to my mind quite clear that before there was any attempt at acceptance by the plaintiff, he was perfectly well aware that Dodds had changed his mind, and that he had in fact agreed to sell the property to Allan. It is impossible, therefore, to say there was ever that existence of the same mind between the two parties which is essential in point of law to the making of an agreement. I am of opinion, therefore, that the plaintiff has failed to prove that there was any binding contract between Dodds and himself.'

Doyle v White City Stadium Ltd [1935] 1 KB 110 Court of Appeal (Lord Hanworth MR, Romer and Slesser LJJ)

Minor - boxing contract

Facts

An infant professional boxer made a contract to fight for £3,000, win, lose or draw. Under the terms of the contract, the fight was subject to the rules of the British Boxing Board of Control. The rules contained a provision that a boxer who was disqualified forfeited his prize money. The infant was disqualified for hitting below the belt and sued for his £3,000.

Held

The rules were, on the whole, for the infant's benefit (they encouraged clean fighting) and, accordingly, he was bound by them. His claim for the £3,000 must fail.

Dunlop Pneumatic Tyre Co Ltd v New Garage and Motor Co Ltd [1915] AC 79 House of Lords (Lords Dunedin, Atkinson, Parker and Parmoor)

Liquidated damages or penalty - question for court

Facts

The appellants manufactured motor tyres and they agreed to supply the respondent retailers on condition that they would not sell at prices below those mentioned in the appellants' price list; if they did, they would pay the appellants £5 for each and every tyre so sold 'as and by way of liquidated damages, and not as a penalty'.

Held

The stipulation was for liquidated damages and the respondents were liable to pay the appellants £5 for each breach of the agreement as to prices.

Eastwood v Kenyon (1840) 11 Ad & El 438 Court of Queen's Bench (Lord Denman CJ, Patteson, Williams and Coleridge JJ)

Consideration - voluntary pecuniary benefit

Facts

S, an infant, inherited a large estate. The plaintiff, S's guardian, spent money on improving the estate and on educating S. When she came of age, she promised to reimburse him. Later, she married the defendant who made a similar promise. The plaintiff sued the defendant on the promise.

Held

The claim would be dismissed as disclosing no cause of action. A pecuniary benefit, voluntarily conferred, is not a sufficient consideration to support a subsequent promise to reimburse. Further, the defendant's promise was not within s4 of the Statute of Frauds.

Edwards v Skyways Ltd [1964] 1 WLR 349 High Court (Megaw J)

Intention to create legal relations?

Facts

As it was necessary to make some of their pilots redundant, the defendants agreed that those concerned, including the plaintiff, would be given an ex gratia payment approximating to the defendants' contributions to their pension fund. Due to their financial difficulties, the defendants failed to make such a payment to the plaintiff: when he sued to recover the amount of the promised ex gratia payment, the defendants maintained that the agreement was not binding as there had been no intention to create legal relations and its terms were too vague.

Held

The plaintiff was entitled to succeed.

Entores Ltd v Miles Far East Corporation [1955] 3 WLR 48 Court of Appeal (Denning, Birkett and Parker LJJ)

Contract - place of acceptance

Facts

An English company in London was in communication with a Dutch company in Amsterdam by telex. The English company received an offer of goods from the Dutch company and made a counter offer which the Dutch company accepted - all by telex. For purposes of jurisdiction, where was the contract made?

Held

In London, where the English company received the acceptance.

Birkett LJ:

> 'I am of opinion that in the case of telex communications (which do not differ in principle from the cases where the parties negotiating a contract are actually in the presence of each other) there can be no binding contract until the offeror receives notice of the acceptance from the offeree. Counsel for the defendants submitted that the proper principle to be applied to a case like the present could be thus stated: "If A makes an offer to B, there is a concluded contract when B has done all that he can do to communicate his acceptance by approved methods." He further submitted that great difficulties would arise if telex communications were treated differently from acceptances by post or telegram.
>
> In my opinion the cases governing the making of contracts by letters passing through the post have no application to the making of contracts by telex communications. The ordinary rule of law, to which the special considerations governing contracts by post are exceptions, is that the acceptance of an offer must be communicated to the offeror and the place where the contract is made is the place where the offeror receives the notification of the acceptance by the offeror. If a telex instrument in Amsterdam is used to send London the notification of the acceptance of an offer, the contract is complete when the telex instrument in London receives the notification of the acceptance (usually at the same moment that the message is being printed in Amsterdam) and the acceptance is then notified to the offeror, and the contract is made in London.'

Evans (J) & Son (Portsmouth) Ltd v Andrea Merzario Ltd [1976] 1 WLR 1078 Court of Appeal (Lord Denning MR, Roskill and Geoffrey Lane LJJ)

Collateral contract - consideration

Facts

The plaintiffs had, from 1959-1967, used the defendants' services as forwarding agents for the import of machines from Italy to England. During that period, the plaintiffs' machines were stored below deck. In 1967, the defendants changed to containers, but orally assured the plaintiffs that the latter's machines would be shipped below deck. On one voyage in 1968, they were not and, due to rough seas, several machines were lost overboard. The defendants sought to rely on their written standard terms which permitted them to carry cargo howsoever they wished and exempted them from liability in the case of loss.

Held

There was a collateral contract between the parties that the plaintiffs' machines would be carried below deck; the plaintiffs furnished consideration for the defendants' promise by entering into the main contract of carriage.

Felthouse v Bindley (1862) 11 CB (NS) 869 Court of Common Pleas (Willes, Byles and Keating JJ); affd (1863) 1 New Rep 401

Offer - 'If I hear no more ...'

Facts

The plaintiff offered to buy his nephew's horse by a letter, in which he said: 'If I hear no more about him, I shall consider the horse mine.' The nephew made no reply to the letter but told the defendant, an auctioneer, that he 'intended to reserve' the horse for his uncle. The defendant inadvertently sold the horse to a third party and the plaintiff sued him.

Held

Since there had been no acceptance of the plaintiff's offer, the plaintiff had no title to sue and the action must fail.

Fibrosa Spolka Akcyjna v Fairbairn Lawson Combe Barbour Ltd [1943] AC 32 House of Lords (Viscount Simon LC, Lords Atkin, Russell of Killowen, Macmillan, Wright, Roche and Porter)

Frustration - goods' place of delivery occupied by enemy

Facts

The defendants, a company in Leeds, contracted in July 1939 to sell machinery to the plaintiffs, a Polish company. On 23 September 1939 Gdynia, the port of delivery, was occupied by the Germans. In July 1939 the plaintiffs had made an advance payment of £1,000 and they now sought its return.

Held

They were entitled to succeed.

Fisher v Bell [1961] 1 QB 394 High Court (Lord Parker CJ, Ashworth and Elvers JJ)

Flick knife offered for sale?

Facts

A flick knife was displayed in a shop window and behind it was a ticket reading 'Ejector knife - 4s'. At that time it was an offence to, inter alia, offer for sale such a knife and the shopkeeper was acquitted of this offence. The prosecutor appealed.

Held

The appeal would be dismissed.

Lord Parker CJ:

'It is clear that, according to the ordinary law of contract, the display of an article with a price on it in a shop window is merely an invitation to treat. It is in no sense an offer for sale the acceptance of which constitutes a contract. That is clearly the general law of the country.'

Flavell, Re, Murray v Flavell (1883) 25 Ch D 89 Court of Appeal (Cotton and Lindley LJJ)

Deceased partner - widow entitled to annuity?

Facts

The defendant was a widow and executrix of the estate of T W Flavell deceased. The deceased was a solicitor who carried on business in partnership. A clause of the partnership agreement provided that the continuing partner pay an annuity to the widow of the retiring or deceased partner. By his will, the deceased devised all his real and personal estate to his wife. He did not, however, direct how the annuity payable under the partnership agreement was to be applied. The question arose whether the annuity payable formed part of the deceased's assets or whether the widow was beneficially entitled to it.

Held

The widow was entitled to the annuity.

Lindley LJ:

'... What kind of a document are we dealing with? It is not a voluntary or fraudulent deed, but a bargain between two partners that if one dies the survivor is to carry on the business, and pay an annuity to be applied for the benefit of the widow. What is the matter with it? It is not fraudulent; it is not a legacy; it is not revocable. It is said to be a voluntary settlement; but if it is, that does not matter if it cannot be impeached. I do not, however, think that it was a voluntary settlement; it was a contract for value. Then it is said that the annuity formed part of the testator's assets, and cannot be diverted from his creditors. The answer is, that it is no part of his assets at all. Unless this contract can be impeached on the ground of fraud, I cannot see why it should not be supported.'

Foakes v Beer (1884) 9 App Cas 605 House of Lords (Earl of Selborne LC, Lords Blackburn, Watson and Fitzgerald)

Judgment debt - payment of smaller sum

Facts

B had obtained judgment against F for £2,000. Sixteen months later, F asked for time to pay and B and F agreed in writing that if F paid £500 immediately and the balance by instalments, B would agree not to take 'any proceedings whatsoever' on the judgment. A judgment debt bears interest from the date of judgment, but the agreement did not mention interest. F finally paid the whole of the outstanding sum and B then claimed interest. B then applied to commence proceedings on the judgment and F pleaded the written agreement as a defence. B argued it was unsupported by consideration.

Held

Following the rule in *Pinnel's Case*, B was entitled to succeed.

The Earl of Selborne LC:

'If the question be (as, in the actual state of the law, I think it is) whether consideration is, or is not, given in a case of this kind, by the debtor who pays down part of the debt presently due from him for a promise by the creditor to relinquish, after further payments on account, the residue of the debt, I cannot say that I think consideration is given, in the sense in which I have always understood that word as used in our law.'

Glasbrook Bros Ltd v Glamorgan County Council [1925] AC 270 House of Lords (Viscount Cave LC, Viscount Finlay, Lords Shaw, Carson and Blanesburgh)

Consideration - duty to protect

Facts

During an industrial dispute, mine owners asked for additional police protection. The police decided that adequate protection could be given by keeping a mobile force on call. The mine owners wanted a permanent billet and agreed to pay for the facility at a specific rate. The appellants (Glasbrook Bros) claimed there was no consideration for the promise, since it was the duty of the council to supply police protection.

Held (Lord Carson and Lord Blanesburgh dissenting)

The council was entitled to recover the agreed sum.

Viscount Finlay:

'The colliery owners repudiated liability on the grounds that there was no consideration for the promise to pay for the police protection and that such an agreement was against public policy. The case was tried by Bailhache J, and he entered judgment for the plaintiffs, saying:

"There is an obligation on the police to afford efficient protection, but if an individual asks for special protection in a particular form, for the special protection so asked for in that particular form, the individual must pay."

This decision was affirmed by a majority on the appeals (Bankes and Scrutton LJJ, Atkin LJ dissenting). The colliery owners now appeal and ask that judgment should be entered for them.

It appears to me that there is nothing in the first point made for the colliery owners that there was no consideration for the promise. It is clear that there was abundant consideration. The police authorities thought that it would be best to give protection by means of a flying column of police, but the colliery owners wanted the "garrison" and promised to pay for it if it was sent.'

Hadley v Baxendale (1854) 9 Ex 341 Court of Exchequer (Parke, Alderson, Platt and Martin BB)

Breach of contract - measure of damages

Facts

The plaintiffs, who were the owners of a flour mill, sent a broken mill shaft, by a well known firm of common carriers, to their suppliers at Greenwich, to provide a pattern for a new shaft. The carrier was slow in delivering the shaft and the plaintiffs claimed damages on the footing that the whole of the activities of the mill were held up for want of the shaft.

Held

There should be a new trial.

NB Because this case is important it is worth quoting at some length the judgment of:

Alderson B:

'Now we think the proper rule in such a case as the present is this: where two parties have made a contract which one of them has broken, the damages which the other party ought to receive in respect of such a breach of contract should be such as may fairly and reasonably be considered either arising naturally, ie according to the usual course of things from such a breach of contract itself, or such as may reasonably be supposed to have been in the contemplation of both parties at the time they made the contract as the probable result of the breach of it. Now, if the special circumstances under which the contract was actually made were communicated by the plaintiffs to the defendants and thus known to both parties, the damages resulting from the breach of such a contract, which they would reasonably contemplate, would be the amount of injury which would ordinarily follow from a breach of contract under these special circumstances so known and communicated. But on the other hand, if those special circumstances were wholly unknown to the party breaking the contract, he, at the most, could only be supposed to have had in his contemplation the amount of injury which would arise generally and in the great multitude of cases not affected by any special circumstances, from such a breach of contract. For, had the special circumstances been known, the parties might have specially provided for the breach of contract by special terms as to the damages in that case; and of this advantage it would be very unjust to deprive them. Now the above principles are those by which we think the jury ought to be guided in estimating the damages arising out of any breach of contract. It is said that other cases, such as breaches of contract in the non-payment of money, or in the not making a good title to land, are to be treated as exceptions from this and as governed by a conventional rule. But as, in such cases, both parties must be supposed to be cognisant of that well known rule, these cases may, we think, be more properly classed under the rule above enunciated as to cases under known special circumstances, because there both parties may reasonably be presumed to contemplate the estimation of the amount of damages according to the conventional rule. Now in the present case, if we are to apply the principles above laid down, we find that the only circumstances here communicated by the plaintiffs to the defendants at the time the contract was made, were that the article to be carried was the broken shaft of a mill and that the plaintiffs were the millers of that mill. But how do all these circumstances show reasonably that the profits of the mill must be stopped by an unreasonable delay in the delivery of the broken shaft by the carrier to the third person? Suppose the plaintiffs had another shaft in their possession, put up or putting up at the time and that they only wished to send back the broken shaft to the engineer who made it; it is clear that this would be quite consistent with the above circumstances and yet the unreasonable delay in the delivery would have no effect upon the intermediate profits of the mill. Or, again, suppose that at the time of the delivery to the carrier, the machinery of the mill had been in other respects defective, then, also, the same results would follow. Here, it is true that the shaft was actually sent back to serve as a model for a new one and that the want of a new one was the only cause of the stoppage of the mill and that the loss of profits really arose from not sending down the new shaft in proper time and that this arose from the delay in delivering the broken one to serve as a model. But it is obvious that in the great multitude of cases of millers sending off broken shafts to third persons by a carrier, under ordinary circumstances such consequences would not, in all probability, have occurred; and these special circumstances were here never communicated by the plaintiffs to the defendants. It follows, therefore, that the loss of profits here cannot reasonably be considered such a consequence of the breach of contract as could have been fairly and reasonably contemplated by both the parties when they made this contract. For such loss would neither have flowed naturally from the breach of this contract in the great multitude of such cases occurring under ordinary circumstances, nor were the special circumstances, which, perhaps, would have made it a reasonable and natural consequence of such breach of contract, communicated to or known by the defendants ...'

Harris v Nickerson (1873) LR 8 QB 286 Queen's Bench (Blackburn, Quain and Archibald JJ)

Advertisement of sale a contract?

Facts

The defendant auctioneer advertised for sale by auction, inter alia, office furniture. The plaintiff travelled to the sale, intending to bid for the office furniture, but these lots were withdrawn from the sale. He sued to recover for two days' loss of time.

Held

His action could not succeed.

Harvela Investments Ltd v Royal Trust Co of Canada (CI) Ltd [1986] AC 207 House of Lords (Lords Fraser of Tullybelton, Diplock, Edmund-Davies, Bridge of Harwich and Templeman)

Sale of shares - sealed bids

Facts

The vendors (the first defendants) invited the plaintiffs and the second defendants to submit, by sealed offer or confidential telex, a single offer for a parcel of shares by a stipulated date. The vendors bound themselves to accept the higher of the two bids and reserved no right to choose between unequal bids. The plaintiffs submitted a bid of C$2,175,000: the second defendants submitted a bid of 'C$2,100,000 or C$101,000 in excess of any other offer, whichever is the higher'. The vendors accepted the second defendants' bid as being a bid of C$2,276,000 and entered into a contract for the sale of the shares.

Held

The second defendants' referential bid was invalid as such bids are inconsistent with a sale by fixed bidding.

Hedley Byrne & Co v Heller & Partners [1964] AC 465 House of Lords (Lords Reid, Morris of Borth-y-Gest, Hodson, Lord Delvin and Pearce)

Negligence - duty of care in relation to information or advice

Facts

The appellants, an advertising agency, wished to make enquiries about the financial reliability of one of their customers, Easipower Ltd. Their bankers made enquiries of the respondents, Easipower's bankers. The respondents replied, first orally then in writing, stating that Easipower Ltd was financially sound, although this information was given 'without responsibility'. The appellants relied on this advice which proved to be inaccurate and they suffered considerable losses when Easipower went into liquidation.

Held

A duty of care in making statements may arise when the parties are in a 'special relationship'. But the appeal was dismissed because the respondents had excluded their responsibility.

See also Chapter 3.

Herne Bay Steam Boat Company v Hutton [1903] 2 KB 683 Court of Appeal (Vaughan Williams, Romer and Stirling LJJ)

Frustration - postponement of Naval Review

Facts

The defendant chartered a boat to take paying passengers to see the Royal Navy Review at Spithead. Upon signing the agreement, the defendant paid a deposit, the balance being due before the boat put out. The Navy Review was postponed and the defendant failed to take the boat out. The plaintiff sued for the balance of the hire fee. The defendant alleged that it was a term of the agreement that the Review should have taken place and that consideration for the agreement had wholly failed.

Held

The plaintiff could recover.

Vaughan William LJ:

'... it could not be said that he could be relieved of his bargain. So, in the present case, it is sufficient to say that the happening of the Naval Review was not the foundation of the contract.'

Hill v C A Parsons & Co Ltd [1971] 3 WLR 995 Court of Appeal (Lord Denning MR, Sachs and Stamp LJJ)

Wrongful dismissal - injunction

Facts

The plaintiff, a chartered engineer aged 63, had been employed by the defendants for 35 years. He was due to retire at 65 and his pension depended on the average salary during the last three years' service. Following a strike, the defendants said that persons of the plaintiff's grade had to join a certain union; he refused and the defendants purported to dismiss him. In his action for wrongful dismissal, he sought an interim injunction.

Held

The injunction would be granted.

Lord Denning MR:

'In these circumstances, it is of the utmost importance to Mr Hill ... that the notice ... should not be held to terminate [his] employment. Damages would not be at all an adequate remedy. If ever there was a case where an injunction should be granted against the employers, this is the case. It is quite plain that the employers have done wrong. I know that the employers have been under pressure from a powerful trade union. That may explain their conduct, but it does not excuse it. They have purported to terminate Mr Hill's employment by a notice which is too short by far. They seek to take advantage of their own wrong by asserting that his services were terminated by their own "say so" at the date selected by them - to the grave prejudice of Mr Hill. They cannot be allowed to break the law in this way. It is, to my mind, a clear case for an injunction.'

Holwell Securities Ltd v Hughes [1974] 1 WLR 155 Court of Appeal (Russell, Buckley and Lawton LJJ)

Offer and acceptance - mode of acceptance prescribed

Facts

The plaintiffs were granted an option to purchase the defendant's freehold property and the agreement provided that the option was exercisable 'by notice in writing to the [defendant] at any time within six months from the date hereof ...' Within that time, the plaintiffs' solicitors wrote to the defendant giving notice of the exercise of the option. The letter was posted, properly addressed and prepaid, but it was never delivered.

Held

The option had not been validly exercised.

Lawton LJ:

'Now in this case, the "notice in writing" was to be one "to the Intending Vendor". It was to be an intimation to him that the grantee had exercised the option: he was the one who was to be fixed with the information contained in the writing. He never was, because the letter carrying the information went astray. The plaintiffs were unable to do what the agreement said they were to do, namely, fix the defendant with knowledge that they had decided to buy his property. If this construction of the option clause is correct, there is no room for the application of any rule of law relating to the acceptance of offers by posting letters since the option agreement stipulated what had to be done to exercise the option. On this ground alone I would dismiss the appeal.'

Hughes v Metropolitan Rail Co (1877) 2 App Cas 439 House of Lords (Lord Cairns LC, Lords O'Hagan, Selborne, Blackburn and Gordon)

Landlord - implied undertaking

Facts

A landlord had given his tenant six months' notice to repair the premises. The lease would be forfeit if the tenant did not comply. The tenant agreed to do the necessary repairs but, at the same time, started negotiations for the sale of the lease to the landlord. The tenant had indicated that the repairs would not be effected while the negotiations were in progress. The negotiations lasted two months, but then broke down. The tenant had carried out no repairs to the premises. When six months from the original notice had expired, the landlord claimed the lease was forfeit.

Held

He was not entitled to forfeiture. The opening of negotiations amounted to a promise by the landlord not to rely on his strict legal rights and enforce the notice and, in reliance on the implied undertaking, the tenant had not carried out the repairs. The six months, therefore, were to run only from the breakdown of the negotiations.

Lord Cairns LC:

'It is the first principle upon which all courts of equity proceed, that if parties who have entered into definite and distinct terms involving certain legal results - certain penalties or legal forfeiture afterwards, by their own act or with their own consent, enter upon a course of negotiations which has the effect of leading one of the parties to suppose that the strict legal rights arising under the contract will not be enforced, or will be kept in suspense or held in abeyance, the person who otherwise might have enforced those rights will not be allowed to enforce them where it would be inequitable, having regard to the dealings which have thus taken place between the parties.'

Hyde v Wrench (1840) 3 Beav 334 Rolls Court (Lord Langdale MR)

Offer - counter offer

Facts

On 6 June, the defendant offered to sell an estate to the plaintiff for £1,000. On 8 June, in reply, the plaintiff made an offer of £950 which was refused by the defendant on 17 June. Finally, on 29 June, the plaintiff wrote purporting to accept the original offer of £1,000.

Held

No contract existed. The counter offer of £950 destroyed the original offer of £1,000 which the plaintiff was incompetent to revive subsequently.

Jackson v Union Marine Insurance Co Ltd (1873) LR 10 CP 125 Court of Exchequer Chamber (Blackburn, Mellor and Lush JJ, Bramwell, Cleasby and Amphlett BB)

Charterparty - consequence of delay

Facts

The plaintiff, a shipowner, entered into a charter party in late 1871. The ship was to proceed from Liverpool to Newport and from Newport to San Francisco with a load of iron rails. The plaintiff insured the freight for the voyage. The ship sailed from Liverpool but ran aground. Six weeks later the charterers chartered another ship. The ship was got off three days later, but repairs would take several months. The issue was whether the plaintiff could maintain an action against the charterers for not loading the ship with the cargo once the ship had been repaired.

Held (Cleasby B dissenting)

The delay put an end to the charter party and the charterers were under no obligation to load the vessel.

Bramwell B:

'If the charter party were read as a charter for a definite adventure, there was necessarily an implied condition that the vessel should arrive at Newport in time for it ... Not arriving in time put an end to the contract, though as it arose from an expected peril, it gave no cause of action.'

Jobson v Johnson [1989] 1 WLR 1026 Court of Appeal (Kerr, Dillon and Nicholls LJJ)

Penalty clause?

Facts

In a sale agreement, in writing, dated 12 August 1982, two brothers agreed to sell 62,666 of their shares in Southend United Football Club Ltd to the defendant's nominee for £40,000. In a side letter written the same day by the defendant and countersigned by the brothers, the defendant agreed to pay a further six half-yearly instalments totalling over £300,000, the payments to begin in February 1984. Paragraph 6 of that side letter made provision for default including the fact that the defendant would, on default, transfer to the brothers shares totalling not less than 44.9 per cent of the issued share capital in the football club, together with variable monetary payments depending on which instalment(s) was/were defaulted. The defendant defaulted at the first instalment. Subsequent arrangements were made for variation of the contract but the defendant, having paid one of the new (varied) instalments again defaulted. The brothers then assigned their rights to the plaintiff who sought to enforce the contract. At first instance Harman J decided that para 6 of the side letter amounted to a penalty clause, but that it was nevertheless enforceable. The defendant appealed.

Held

i) Whether a clause was a penalty clause was a question of construction, to be decided in the light of the circumstances at the time of making the contract and in the present case, since para 6 provided for repurchase of the shares at a fixed price regardless of the extent of the defendant's default, it amounted to a penalty clause.

ii) (Kerr LJ dissenting) the penalty clause was unenforceable to the extent that it provided for compensation to the innocent party in excess of his actual loss.

Nicholls LJ:

'Although in practice a penalty clause in a contract ... is effectively a dead letter, it is important in the present case to note that, contrary to the submissions of counsel for the defendant, the strict legal position is not that such a clause is simply struck out of the contract, as though with a blue pencil, so that the contract takes effect as if it had never been included therein. Strictly, the legal position is that the clause remains in the contract and can be sued on, but it will not be enforced by the court beyond the sum which represents, in the events which have happened, the actual loss of the party seeking payment. There are many cases which make this clear.'

Johnson v Agnew [1980] AC 367 House of Lords (Lords Wilberforce, Salmon, Fraser, Keith and Scarman)

Damages - date of assessment

Facts

In November 1973 the parties contracted for the sale and purchase of a house and land, the properties being mortgaged separately. The purchaser paid part of the deposit and accepted the vendor's title but did not complete by 6 December, the contract date. On 21 December the vendors gave notice that 21 January 1974 was the final date for completion, but the purchaser failed to complete and on 8 March the vendors commenced proceedings. An order for specific performance was made on 27 June, although it was not entered until 26 November, by which time the mortgagees of the house had obtained an order for possession. In March 1975 the land mortgagees obtained such an order and on 3 April and 20 June respectively the land and house mortgagees contracted sales, completions taking place in July.

Held

The vendors were entitled not only to an order discharging the specific performance order but also to damages for breach of contract assessed at 3 April 1975.

See also Chapter 1.

Kleinwort Benson Ltd v Malaysia Mining Corp Bhd [1989] 1 WLR 379 Court of Appeal (Fox, Ralph Gibson and Nicholls LJJ)

Letter of comfort - contractual effect?

Facts

The plaintiff bank negotiated with the defendants for the making of loan facility of up to £10m available to the defendants' wholly-owned subsidiary MMC Metals Ltd ('Metals'). The plaintiffs having sought from the defendants assurances as to the responsibility of the defendants for the repayment by Metals of any sums lent by the plaintiffs, the defendants provided a comfort letter containing the statement (in para 3): 'It is our policy to ensure that the business of [Metals] is at all times in a position to meet its liabilities to you under the ... arrangements.' Metals went into liquidation owing the whole amount of the facility and the plaintiffs sought payment from the defendants.

Held

Their action would fail as, on the facts, the letter gave rise to no more than a moral responsibility on the defendants' part to meet Metals' debt.

Koufos v C Czarnikow Ltd (The Heron II) [1969] AC 350 House of Lords (Lords Reid, Morris of Borth-y-Gest, Hodson, Pearce and Upjohn)

Damages - loss of profit

Facts

By a charter party made in London in October 1960 between Nomicos Ltd, as agents for the appellant (the owner of the Heron II) and the respondent charterers, the charterers chartered the Heron II, then in Piraeus expected ready to load 25-27 October all being well to proceed to Constanza and there load a consignment of 3,000 metric tons of sugar and proceed with all convenient speed to Basrah. Lay days were not to commence before 27 October and if the ship was not ready to load by 10 November, the charterers had the option of cancelling the charter party. The charterers also had the option of discharging the cargo at Jeddah. The vessel did load as expected and began the voyage to Basrah, a voyage of approximately 20 days. The vessel deviated from the voyage by calling at Berbera for three days, where she loaded livestock and fodder for Bahrein. The vessel again deviated from the voyage when she called at Bahrein to discharge the livestock and fodder. She stayed there for three days. A third deviation was made, to call at Abadan, for one day. These deviations were made without the knowledge or consent of the charterers. The voyage was prolonged by nine days in all as a result. At all times, the charterers intended to sell the sugar for cash, promptly on arrival. They did so. The shipowners admitted that they were in breach of the charter party and the charterers contended that if the sugar had arrived even five days earlier, it would have commanded a higher price. It was found as a fact that there was, at all material times, a market for sugar in Basrah and the prices fluctuated considerably. The existence of the market was known to the shipowners at all material times, but they did not have any detailed knowledge of it. It was generally known that sugar was a perishable commodity and that there was some urgency in carrying it. However, the fall in the price had been caused by the arrival of a large consignment at Basrah four days earlier. This was nothing unusual or unpredictable. The umpire appointed by the arbitrator held that the charterers were entitled to recover as damages the difference between the price of the sugar when it should have been delivered, and the price when it was in fact delivered. The shipowners appealed and McNair J held that the charterers were only entitled to recover as damages interest on the value of the cargo during the period of delay, plus expenses. The charterers appealed and the Court of Appeal restored the umpire's award. The shipowners then appealed.

Held

Loss of profit was recoverable as damages.

Krell v Henry [1903] 2 KB 740 Court of Appeal (Vaughan Williams, Romer and Stirling LJJ)

Frustration - cancellation of procession

Facts

In 1902, the defendant hired from the plaintiff, a flat in Pall Mall for two days for the purpose of viewing the coronation processions. The King became ill and the coronation was cancelled. The plaintiff sued for the agreed hire charge.

Held

The contract was a licence to use the rooms for a particular purpose and, as the foundation of the licence was destroyed, the contract was frustrated.

Leeds Industrial Co-operative Society v Slack [1924] AC 851 House of Lords (Earl of Birkenhead, Viscount Finley, Lords Dunedin, Sumner and Carson)

Injunction - award of damages in lieu

Facts

The parties owned premises on opposite sides of a narrow passage. The defendants demolished theirs and commenced rebuilding: the plaintiffs maintained that the new building already had, and when completed would even more, infringe their right to light and they sought an injunction. At the date of the trial, it was found that the new building had not yet interfered unlawfully with the plaintiffs' ancient lights.

Held (Lord Sumner and Lord Carson dissenting)

An award of damages could be made in lieu of an injunction and the measure of damages would be the damage to be sustained following completion of the building.

Lumley v Wagner (1852) 1 De GM & G 604 Lord Chancellor's Court (Lord St Leonards LC)

Injunction - contract for personal services

Facts

The defendant cantatrice bound herself to sing for three months at the plaintiff's London theatre and 'not to use her talents' at any other place during that time.

Held

An injunction could be granted to restrain her from appearing at another theatre.

Lord St Leonards LC:

'It was objected that the operation of the injunction in the present case was mischievous, excluding the defendant Johanna Wagner from performing at any other theatre while this court had no power to compel her to perform at Her Majesty's Theatre. It is true that I have not the means of compelling her to sing, but she has no cause of complaint if I compel her to abstain from the commission of an act which she has bound herself not to do, and thus possibly cause her to fulfil her engagement. The jurisdiction which I now exercise is wholly within the power of the court, and, being of opinion that it is a proper case for interfering, I shall leave nothing unsatisfied by the judgment I pronounce. The effect, too, of the injunction, in restraining Johanna Wagner from singing elsewhere may, in the event of an action being brought against her by the plaintiff, prevent any such amount of vindictive damages being given against her as a jury might probably be inclined to give if she had carried her talents and exercised them at the rival theatre. The injunction may also, as I have said, tend to the fulfilment of her engagement, though, in continuing the injunction, I disclaim doing indirectly what I cannot do directly.'

McArdle, Re [1951] Ch 669 Court of Appeal (Sir Raymond Evershed MR, Jenkins and Hodson LJJ)

Consideration - past

Facts

A number of children were entitled to a house after their mother's death. During the mother's life, one of the children and his wife lived with her in the house and the wife made various improvements to the house. At a later date, all the children signed a document addressed to her, stating that 'in consideration' of these improvements, on the mother's death the wife would be entitled to £488 from the estate (being the amount spent on the improvements).

Held

This was a case of past consideration and the promise was merely gratuitous, since the work had already been done.

McRae v Commonwealth Disposals Commission (1951) 84 CLR 377 High Court of Australia (Dixon, Fullagar and McTieman JJ)

Contractor - purchase of non-existent tanker

Facts

The defendants invited tenders for an oil tanker, loaded with oil, lying on Jourmand Reef off Papua. The plaintiff's tender was accepted and he incurred considerable expense in going to retrieve the vessel and its contents. There was no ship to be found where the vessel was supposed to be - and no place known as Jourmand Reef. The plaintiff claimed, inter alia, damages for breach of contract.

Held

He was entitled to succeed.

Dixon and Fullagar JJ:

> 'The position ... may be summed up as follows: It was not decided in *Couturier* v *Hastie* that the contract in that case was void. The question whether it was void or not did not arise. If it had arisen, as in an action by the purchaser for damages, it would have turned on the ulterior question whether the contract was subject to an implied condition precedent. Whatever might then have been held on the facts of *Couturier* v *Hastie*, it is impossible in this case to imply any such term. The terms of the contract and the surrounding circumstances clearly exclude any such implication. The buyers relied upon, and acted upon, the assertion of the seller that there was a tanker in existence. It is not a case in which the parties can be seen to have proceeded on the basis of a common assumption of fact so as to justify the conclusion that the correctness of the assumption was intended by both parties to be a condition precedent to the creation of contractual obligation. The officers of the Commission made an assumption, but the plaintiffs did not make an assumption in the same sense. They knew nothing except what the Commission had told them. If they had been asked, they would certainly not have said: "Of course, if there is no tanker, there is no contract." They would have said: "We shall have to go and take possession of the tanker. We simply accept the Commission's assurance that there is a tanker and the Commission's promise to give us that tanker." The only proper construction of the contract is that it included a promise by the Commission that there was a tanker in the position specified. The Commission contracted that there was a tanker there ... If, on the other hand, the case of *Couturier* v *Hastie* and this case ought to be treated as cases raising a question of "mistake", then the Commission cannot in this case rely on any mistake as avoiding the contract, because any mistake was induced by the serious fault of their own servants, who asserted the existence of a tanker recklessly and without any reasonable ground. There *was* a contract, and the Commission contracted that a tanker existed in the position specified. Since there was no such tanker, there has been a breach of contract, and the plaintiffs are entitled to damages for that breach.
>
> Before proceeding to consider the measure of damages one other matter should be briefly mentioned. The contract was made in Melbourne, and it would seem that its proper law is Victorian law. Section 11 of the Victorian Goods Act 1928, corresponds to s6 of the English Sale of Goods Act 1893, and provides that "where there is a contract for the sale of specified goods, and the goods without the knowledge of the seller have perished at the time when the contract is made the contract is void". This has been generally supposed to represent the legislature's view of the effect of *Couturier* v *Hastie*. Whether it correctly represents the effect of the decision in that case or not, it seems clear that the section has no application to the facts of the present case. Here the goods never existed and the seller ought to have known that they did not exist.'

Maple Flock Co Ltd v Universal Furniture Products (Wembley) Ltd [1934] 1 KB 148
Court of Appeal (Lord Hewart CJ, Lord Wright and Slesser LJ)

Sale of goods - defect in one instalment

Facts

There was a contract between the parties for the sale of 100 tons of flock, delivery to be made in three loads a week as required. One instalment of one and half tons was defective, but there was no reasonable probability that there would be anything wrong with future deliveries.

Held

The buyers were not entitled to treat the contract as having been repudiated by the sellers.

Lord Hewart CJ:

'There may, indeed, be ... cases where the consequences of single breach of contract may be so serious as to involve a frustration of the contract and justify rescission, or, furthermore, the contract might contain an express condition that a breach would justify rescission, in which case effect would be given to such a condition by the court. But none of these circumstances can be predicated of this case. We think the deciding factor here is the extreme improbability of the breach being repeated, and on that ground, and on the isolated and limited character of the breach complained of, there was, in our judgment, no sufficient justification to entitle the respondents to refuse further deliveries as they did.'

Mareva Compania Naviera SA v International Bulk Carriers SA, The Mareva [1980] 1 All ER 213 Court of Appeal (Lord Denning MR, Roskill and Ormrod LJJ)

Injunction - danger of transfer of assets out of jurisdiction

Facts

The plaintiffs sought, inter alia, damages for alleged repudiation of a charter-party and, on an ex parte application, a judge had granted an injunction restraining the defendants from removing or disposing out of the jurisdiction monies in their London bank account.

Held

The injunction would be extended.

Lord Denning MR:

'... Section 45 of the Supreme Court of Judicature (Consolidation) Act 1925 says:

"A mandamus or an injunction may be granted or a receiver appointed by an interlocutory Order of the Court in all cases in which it shall appear to the Court to be just or convenient ..."

In *Beddow* v *Beddow* Jessel MR gave a very wide interpretation to that section. He said: "I have unlimited power to grant an injunction in any case where it would be right or just to do so ..."

There is only one qualification to be made. The court will not grant an injunction to protect a person who has no legal or equitable right whatever ... But, subject to that qualification, the statute gives a wide general power to the courts. It is well summarised in Halsbury's Laws of England:

"... now, therefore, whenever a right, which can be asserted either at law or in equity, does not exist, then whatever the previous practice may have been, the Court is enabled by virtue of this provision, in a proper case, to grant an injunction to protect that right."'

Maritime National Fish Ltd v Ocean Trawlers Ltd [1935] AC 524 Privy Council (Lords Atkin, Tomlin, Macmillan and Wright)

Frustration - act of party setting up

Facts

The defendants operated a fleet of trawlers for fishing. Three were owned and two were chartered. One was chartered from the plaintiffs. A government licence was required to operate the trawlers. The defendants were only able to secure three licences. The defendants allocated two licences to two of their own trawlers and the third to the trawler not chartered from the plaintiffs. The defendants argued that the charter was frustrated.

Held

The charter was not frustrated as it was self-induced by the act and election of the defendants.

Lord Wright:

'The essence of frustration is that it should not be due to the act or election of the party. There does not appear to be any authority which has been directly decided on this point. There is, however, a reference to the question in the speech of Lord Sumner in *Bank Line Ltd v Arthur Capel and Co* [1919] AC 435. What he says is:

"One matter I mention only to get rid of it. When the ship-owners were first applied to by the Admiralty for a ship, they named three, of which the Quito was one, and intimated that she was the one they preferred to give up. I think it is now well settled that the principle of frustration of an adventure assumes that the frustration arises without blame or fault on either side. Reliance cannot be placed on a self-induced frustration. Indeed, such conduct might give the other clear party the option to treat the contract as repudiated ..."

However, the point does arise in the facts now before the Board and their Lordships are of the opinion that the loss of the St Cuthbert's licence can correctly be described, quoad the appellants, as a "self-induced frustration".'

Nash v Inman [1908] 2 KB 1 Court of Appeal (Sir Herbert Cozens-Hardy MR, Fletcher Moulton and Buckley LJJ)

Minor - fancy waistcoats

Facts

A tailor commenced proceedings to recover £122.19s.6d for clothes, including eleven fancy waistcoats, supplied to an infant Cambridge undergraduate.

Held

That the action must fail, as the evidence showed that the infant already had sufficient clothing suitable to his position.

Fletcher Moulton LJ:

'An infant, like a lunatic, is incapable of making a contract of purchase in the strict sense of the words; but if a man satisfies the needs of the infant or lunatic by supplying to him necessaries, the law will imply an obligation to repay him for the services so rendered and will enforce that obligation ... That the articles were necessaries had to be alleged and proved by the plaintiff as part of his case and the sum he recovered was based on a quantum meruit. If he claimed anything beyond this he failed and it did not help him that he could prove that the prices were agreed prices. All that is ... confirmed by the provision of section 2 of the Sale of Goods Act 1893 - an Act which was intended to codify the existing law. That section expressly provides that the consequence of necessaries sold and delivered to an infant is that he must pay a reasonable price therefor ...'

New Zealand Shipping Co Ltd v A M Satterthwaite and Co Ltd, The Eurymedon [1975] AC 154 Privy Council (Viscount Dilhorne, Lords Wilberforce, Hodson, Simon of Glaisdale and Salmon)

Contract of carriage - exclusion clause

Facts

The consignor loaded goods on a ship for carriage to the plaintiff consignee in New Zealand. The carriage was subject to a bill of lading containing the following:

'it is hereby expressly agreed that no servant or agent of the carrier (including every independent contractor from time to time employed by the carrier) shall in any circumstances whatsoever be under any liability whatsoever to the shipper, consignee or owner of the goods or to any holder of the bill of lading for any loss or damage or delay of whatsoever kind arising or resulting directly or indirectly from any neglect or default on his part while acting in the course of or in connection with his employment and, without prejudice to the generality of the foregoing provisions in this clause, every exemption, limitation, condition and liberty herein contained and every right, exemption from liability, defence and immunity of whatsoever nature applicable to the carrier as to which the carrier is entitled hereunder shall also be available and shall extend to protect every such servant or agent of the carrier acting as aforesaid and for the purpose of all the foregoing provisions of this clause, the carrier is, or shall be, deemed to be acting as agent or trustee on behalf of and for the benefit of all persons who are or might be his servants or agents from time to time (including independent contractors as aforesaid) and all such persons shall to this extent be or deemed to be parties to the contract in or evidenced by this bill of lading.'

The cargo was damaged as a result of the negligence of the defendant stevedores, who had been employed by the carriers to unload the cargo. The plaintiffs, the holder of the bill of loading, sued for damage by negligence. The defendant pleaded the clause contained in the bill of lading.

Held (Viscount Dilhorne and Lord Simon of Glaisdale dissenting)

The defendant could rely on the clause and, accordingly, the action was dismissed.

Page One Records Ltd v Britton [1968] 1 WLR 157 High Court (Stamp J)

Injunction - contract for personal services

Facts

The defendant musicians ('The Troggs') appointed the plaintiffs their manager for five years. During that time, they sought an interlocutory injunction to restrain them from engaging any other manager.

Held

The injunction would be refused.

Stamp J:

'... it was said in this case, that if an injunction is granted The Troggs could, without employing any other manager or agent, continue as a group on their own or seek other employment of a different nature. So far as the former suggestion is concerned, in the first place, I doubt whether consistently with the terms of the agreements which I have read, The Troggs could act as their own managers; and, in the second place, I think that I can and should take judicial notice of the fact that these groups, if they are to have any great success, must have managers. Indeed, it is the plaintiffs' own case that The Troggs are simple persons, of no business experience, and could not survive without the services of a manager. As a practical matter on the evidence before me, I entertain no doubt that they would be compelled, if the injunction were granted on the terms that the plaintiffs seek, to continue to employ the first plaintiff as their manager and agent and it is, I think, on this point that this case diverges from the *Lumley* v *Wagner* case ... and the cases which have followed it, including the *Warner Brothers* case: for it would be a bad thing to put pressure on The Troggs to continue to employ as a manager and agent in a fiduciary capacity one, who, unlike the plaintiff in those cases who had merely to pay the defendant money, has duties of a personal and fiduciary nature to perform and in whom The Troggs, for reasons good, bad or indifferent, have lost confidence and who may for all I know, fail in its duty to them.

On the facts before me on this interlocutory motion, I should, if I granted the injunction, be enforcing a contract for personal services in which personal services are to be performed by the first plaintiff. In *Lumley* v *Wagner*, Lord St Leonards LC in his judgment, disclaimed doing indirectly what he could not do directly; and in the present case, by granting an injunction I would, in my judgment, be doing precisely that. I must therefore, refuse the injunction.'

Pao On v Lau Yiu Long [1980] AC 614 Privy Council (Viscount Dilhorne, Lords Wilberforce, Simon of Glaisdale, Salmon and Scarman)

Consideration - duress

Facts

The plaintiffs owned a private company ('Shing On') and the defendants were majority shareholders in Fu Chip, a public investment company. By a written agreement dated 27 February 1973, the plaintiffs contracted to sell Shing On's shares to Fu Chip, the price being an allotment of Fu Chip shares at a deemed value of $2.50 a share: the plaintiffs undertook that they would not sell 2.5 million of the shares allotted to them before the end of April 1974. By a subsidiary agreement of the same date, the defendants agreed to buy back, on or before 30 April 1974, 2.5 million Fu Chip shares at $2.50 a share. As it was generally expected that the Fu Chip shares would rise in value, the plaintiffs realised that they had made a bad bargain and they told the defendants that they would not complete the main agreement unless the subsidiary agreement was replaced by an agreement guaranteeing the price of the 2.5 million shares at $2.50 a share. Anxious to complete the main agreement, but knowing that they could claim specific performance of it, the defendants, wishing to avoid litigation, agreed. By 30 April 1974 Fu Chip's share price had fallen to 36 cents: the plaintiffs sought to enforce the guarantee. Before the Board, the questions for decision were: was there consideration for the contract of guarantee? If there was, was the defendant's consent vitiated by duress?

Held

The plaintiffs were entitled to succeed.

Parsons (H) (Livestock) Ltd v Uttley, Ingham & Co Ltd [1977] 3 WLR 990 Court of Appeal (Lord Denning MR, Orr and Scarman LJJ)

Breach of contract - damages recoverable

Facts

The plaintiff pig farmers bought from the defendant manufacturers a second bulk food storage hopper 'fitted with ventilated top'. In transporting the hopper to the farm the defendants sealed down the ventilator to stop it rattling. They forgot to unseal it (which the plaintiffs could not have detected as it was 28 feet above the ground); the pig nuts became mouldy, the pigs became ill from a rare type of infection and 254 of them died. The plaintiffs sued for damages.

Held

They were entitled to succeed and to recover by way of damages the losses sustained from the death and sickness of the pigs.

Partridge v Crittenden [1968] 1 WLR 1204 High Court (Lord Parker CJ, Ashworth and Blain JJ)

Brambling offered for sale?

Facts

It was an offence to offer for sale certain wild birds, including bramblings. Under the heading 'Classified Advertisements' in the periodical Cage and Aviary Birds, the appellant had advertised 'Quality Bramblefinch cocks, Bramblefinch hens, 25s each'.

Held

His conviction of this offence would be quashed.

Lord Parker CJ:

'I agree [that the conviction should be quashed] and with less reluctance than in *Fisher* v *Bell* [1961] 1 QB 394 ... I say "with less reluctance" because I think that when one is dealing with advertisements and circulars, unless they indeed come from manufacturers, there is business sense in their being construed as invitations to treat and not offers for sale. In a very different context Lord Herschell in *Grainger & Son* v *Gough (Surveyor of Taxes)* [1896] AC 325, said this in dealing with a price list:

"The transmission of such a price list does not amount to an offer to supply an unlimited quantity of the wine described at the price named, so that as soon as an order is given there is a binding contract to supply that quantity. If it were so, the merchant might find himself involved in any number of contractual obligations to supply wine of a particular description which he would be quite unable to carry out, his stock of wine of that description being necessarily limited."

Payne v Cave (1789) 3 Term Rep 148 Court of King's Bench (Lord Kenyon CJ, Ashhurst, Buller and Grose JJ)

Auction sale - when contract concluded

Facts

Goods were put up for sale by auction and the defendant was the last bidder. Before the goods were knocked down to him, the defendant purported to withdraw his bid.

Held

He was entitled to do so. 'Every bidding is nothing more than an offer on one side which is not binding on either side till it is assented to. But according to what is now contended for [by the plaintiff], one party would be bound by the offer and the other not, which can never be allowed.'

Commentary

See now s57(2) of the Sale of Goods Act 1979.

Payzu Ltd v Saunders [1919] 2 KB 581 Court of Appeal (Bankes and Scrutton LJJ and Eve J)

Breach of contract - duty to mitigate loss

Facts

The defendant, having agreed to sell the plaintiffs 200 pieces of silk, delivered the final consignment for which the plaintiffs failed to pay punctually. In view of this, the defendant said that she would only deliver further supplies if the plaintiffs paid on delivery. This the plaintiffs would not accept, so they sued for breach of contract, claiming the differences between the contract price and the current market price.

Held

Although the defendant was liable, the plaintiffs' failure to pay promptly for the first consignment not amounting to a repudiation of the contract, the plaintiffs should have mitigated their loss by accepting her cash-on-delivery terms and they were entitled to recover only the amount which they would have lost had they done so.

Scrutton LJ:

'Whether it be more correct to say that a plaintiff must minimise his damages, or to say that he can recover no more than he would have suffered if he had acted reasonably, because any further damages do not reasonably follow from the defendant's breach, the result is the same. The plaintiff must take "all reasonable steps to mitigate the loss consequent on the breach" and this simple principle "debars him from claiming any part of the damage which is due to his neglect to take such steps": *British Westinghouse Electric and Manufacturing Co v Underground Electric Railways Co of London Ltd* ... per Lord Haldane LC. Counsel for the plaintiffs has contended that in considering what steps should be taken to mitigate the damage all contractual relations with the party in default must be excluded. That is contrary to my experience. In certain cases of personal service it may be unreasonable to expect a plaintiff to consider an offer from the other party who has grossly injured him; but in commercial contracts it is generally reasonable to accept an offer from the party in default. However, it is always a question of fact. About the law there is no difficulty.'

Pharmaceutical Society of Great Britain v Boots Cash Chemists (Southern) Ltd
[1953] 1 QB 401 Court of Appeal (Somervell, Birkett and Romer LJJ)

Supermarket - when contract of sale concluded

Facts

Statute required that sales of certain poisons should be supervised by a registered pharmacist. A customer took one such poison off the shelf of a 'self-service' shop or supermarket and the transaction was supervised by a pharmacist at the cash desk.

Held

No offence had been committed because there had been no sale until the customer's money had been taken at the cash desk.

Somervell LJ:

'I agree entirely ... that in the case of the ordinary shop, although goods are displayed and it is intended that customers should go and choose what they want, the contract is not completed until the customer has indicated the article which he needs and the shopkeeper or someone on his behalf accepts that offer. Not till then is the contract completed, and, that being the normal position, I can see no reason for drawing any different inference from the arrangements which were made in the present case ...

I can see no reason for implying from this arrangement any position other than that ... it is a convenient method of enabling customers to see what there is for sale, to choose and, possibly, to put back and substitute, articles which they wish to have, and then go to the cashier and offer to buy what they have chosen. On that conclusion the case fails, because it is admitted that in those circumstances there was supervision in the sense required by the Act and at the appropriate moment of time.'

Pinnel's Case (1602) 5 Co Rep 117a Court of Common Pleas

Payment of part

Facts

The plaintiff sued for £8 10s and the defendant pleaded that, before the date when the payment was due, he had paid the plaintiff £5 2s 2d which he (the plaintiff) had accepted in full satisfaction of the £8 10s.

Held

The plaintiff was entitled to judgment because of the defendant's 'insufficient pleading'. However, the whole court resolved that: "the payment and acceptance of parcel [part] before the day in satisfaction of the whole, would be a good satisfaction in regard of circumstance of time; for peradventure parcel of it before the day would be more beneficial to him than the whole at the day, and the value of the satisfaction is not material. So if I am bound in £20 to pay you £10 at Westminster and you request me to pay you £5 at the day at York, and you will accept it in full satisfaction of the whole £10 it is a good satisfaction for the whole for the expense to pay it at York, is sufficient satisfaction. The court also resolved that payment of a lesser sum on the day in satisfaction of a greater, cannot be any satisfaction for the whole, because it appears to the judges that by no possibility a lesser sum can be a satisfaction to the plaintiff for a greater sum; but the gift of a horse, hawk or robe, etc, in satisfaction is good, for it shall be intended that a horse, hawk or robe, etc, might be more beneficial to the plaintiff than the money, in respect of some circumstance, or otherwise the plaintiff would not have accepted of it in satisfaction. But when the whole sum is due, by no intendment the acceptance of parcel can be a satisfaction to the plaintiff.'

Pioneer Shipping Ltd v BTP Tioxide Ltd, The Nema [1982] AC 724 House of Lords (Lords Diplock, Fraser of Tullybelton, Russell of Killowen, Keith of Kinkel and Roskill)

Charter-party - frustration by strikes

Facts

Owners of a vessel chartered her for six or seven consecutive voyages from Sorel in Canada to ports in Europe between April and December. A strike broke out at Sorel while the vessel was away on the first of these voyages and it was still in progress when she arrived back there, thus preventing loading for the second voyage. It was agreed, therefore, that the owners could send the ship on a voyage to Glasgow: the owners sought to extend this voyage, but the charterers refused. The owners nevertheless arranged for the vessel to go to Brazil and Portugal, maintaining that the charter party had been frustrated, a view which the arbitrator supported.

Held

The arbitrator's decision would not be disturbed.

It was not suggested that a strike could never bring about frustration of an adventure. But it was pointed out that most attempts to invoke strikes as a cause of frustration have in the past failed. *The Penelope* is almost the only example of success, and in that case the underlying reasoning of the judgment is far from easy to follow, even though the decision may well be correct.

> 'My Lords, I see no reason in principle why a strike should not be capable of causing frustration of an adventure by delay. It cannot be right to divide causes of delay into classes and then say that one class can and another class cannot bring about frustration of an adventure. It is not the nature of the cause of delay which matters so much as the effect of that cause on the performance of the obligations which the parties have assumed one towards the other.'

Planché v Colburn (1831) 8 Bing 14 Court of Common Pleas (Tindal CJ, Gaselee, Bosanquet and Alderson JJ)

Literary work abandoned - author's entitlement

Facts

The plaintiff agreed with the defendant publishers to contribute, for £100, a volume on costume and ancient armour for 'The Juvenile Library'. After the plaintiff had begun work, the defendants abandoned the series. The plaintiff sued for breach of contract and he was awarded £50 damages.

Held

This verdict would not be disturbed.

Bosanquet J:

> 'The plaintiff is entitled to retain his verdict. The jury have found that the contract was abandoned but it is said that the plaintiff ought to have tendered or delivered the work. It was part of the contract, however, that the work should be published in a particular shape and if it had been delivered

after the abandonment of the original design, it might have been published in a way not consistent with the plaintiff's reputation, or not at all.'

Posner v Scott-Lewis [1986] 3 WLR 531 High Court (Mervyn Davies J)

Specific performance - personal services

Facts

Under the terms of the leases of the plaintiff tenants at Danes Court, the defendant landlord was obliged to employ a resident porter to keep the communal area clean, to be responsible for the boiler and to collect rubbish from the flats. The resident porter left, but continued to do the work on a part-time basis. If the defendant was thereby in breach of the covenant, could the covenant be specifically enforced?

Held

The defendant was in breach and the court could and would make an order for specific performance.

Mervyn Davies J:

'Drawing attention to ... differences between [*Ryan* v *Mutual Tontine Westminster Chambers Association* [1893] 1 Ch 116] and the present case, counsel for the plaintiffs submitted that *Ryan's Case* should be distinguished, in short, he said that since the resident porter's functions at Danes Court were already obligations of the lessor to the lessees, there were no duties on the part of the porter towards the tenants that the tenants were seeking to enforce. All that was required was the appointment of a resident porter, whereas in *Ryan's Case* the plaintiff was in effect seeking to enforce performance of duties said to be owed by the porter to the plaintiff. I do not accept or reject counsel for the plaintiffs' able argument. I suspect that it is difficult to distinguish *Ryan's Case*. However that may be, *Ryan's Case* has been remarked on in many later authorities.'

R v Clarke (1927) 40 CLR 227 High Court of Australia (Isaacs ACJ, Higgins and Starke JJ)

Offer - information given for other reasons

Facts

A reward had been offered for information leading to the arrest and conviction of the murderer of two police officers. Clarke, who knew of the offer and was himself suspected of the crime, gave such information. He admitted that he had done so only to clear himself of the charge and at the time he gave the information, all thought of the reward had passed out of his mind.

Held

He was not entitled to the reward.

Higgins J:

'Clarke had seen the offer, indeed; but it was not present to his mind - he had forgotten it, and gave no consideration to it, in his intense excitement as to his own danger. There cannot be assent without knowledge of the offer.'

Reardon Smith Line Ltd v Yngvar Hansen-Tangen [1976] 1 WLR 989 House of Lords (Viscount Dilhorne, Lords Wilberforce, Simon of Glaisdale, Kilbrandon and Russell of Killowen)

Charter - words of identification or contractual description?

Facts

In order to perform a charter, a steamship company nominated a vessel 'to be built by Osaka Shipbuilding Co Ltd and known as Hull No 354 until named'. Osaka was unable to build the ship in its own yard and so subcontracted the work to Oshima, a newly created company in which it held 50 per cent of the shares. Osaka provided a large part of Oshima's work force and managerial staff. In Osaka's books the ship was numbered 354; in Oshima's 004. Although the vessel when built complied fully with the physical specifications in the charter and was fit for the contemplated service, delivery was refused.

Held

The charterers were not entitled to refuse delivery.

Reid v Commissioner of Police of the Metropolis [1973] QB 551 Court of Appeal (Lord Denning MR, Phillimore and Scarman LJJ)

Sale in market overt - time

Facts

The plaintiff's Adam candelabra had been stolen and the second defendant had bought them, before sunrise, from an unknown dealer in New Caledonian Market, a market constituted under statute. The plaintiff sought their return.

Held

He was entitled to succeed as the second defendant had not bought the goods in market overt.

Phillimore LJ:

> 'The phase market overt has two meanings, first the literal meaning namely "open market" and, second a meaning well understood by lawyers, namely, the circumstances in which a sale in a market conveys a good title to the purchaser even against the true owner. At common law title could only be conveyed as against the true owner subject to various safeguards. These are clearly stated in Coke's Institutes. The vital excerpt for the purposes of the present case is no 11 which stipulates, inter alia, that the sale can only convey title against the true owner if it takes place between sunrise and sunset.
>
> In *Bishopsgate Motor Finance Corpn Ltd* v *Transport Brakes Ltd* [1949] 1 KB 322, this court held that the doctrine of market overt applies to a market created by statute just as it has always done at common law to markets established by grant of a charter or by prescription. It is, I think, quite clear that the court intended that if title was to pass as against the true owner the transaction must be subject to the same safeguards as are described by Coke.'

Roscorla v Thomas (1842) 3 QB 234 Queen's Bench (Lord Denman CJ)

Consideration - past

Facts

In an action for breach of warranty as to the soundness of a horse, the declaration stated that in consideration that the plaintiff, at the request of the defendant, had bought of the defendant a horse for the sum of £30, the defendant promised that it was sound and free from vice. It was argued for the defendant that the precedent executed consideration was insufficient to support the subsequent promise.

Held

This was the case.

Lord Denman CJ:

'It may be taken as a general rule, subject to exceptions not applicable to this case, that the promise must be co-extensive with the consideration. In the present case, the only promise that would result from the consideration as stated and be co-extensive with it, would be to deliver the horse upon request.'

Rose & Frank Co v J R Crompton & Bros Ltd [1925] AC 445 House of Lords (Earl of Birkenhead, Lords Atkinson, Sumner, Buckmaster and Phillimore)

Contract - intention not to be legally enforceable

Facts

A contract between the parties relating to carbonising tissue paper concluded with a clause as follows:

'This arrangement is not entered into, nor is this memorandum written, as a formal or legal agreement, and shall not be subject to legal jurisdiction in the law courts either of the United States or England, but it is only a definite expression and record of the purpose and intention of the three parties concerned, to which they each honourably pledge themselves with the fullest confidence - based on past business with each other - that it will be carried through by each of the three parties with mutual loyalty and friendly co-operation.'

One of the parties to the agreement sued another for damages for breach of contract.

Held

The action could not succeed as the parties to the agreement had not intended it to be legally enforceable.

Lord Phillimore:

'It is true that when the tribunal has before it for construction an instrument which unquestionably creates a legal interest and the dispute is only to the quality and extent of that interest, then later repugnant clauses in the instrument cutting down that interest which the earlier part of it has given are to be rejected, but this doctrine does not apply when the question is whether it is intended to create any legal interest at all. Here, I think, the overriding clause in the document is that which provided that it is to be a contract of honour only and unenforceable at law.'

Routledge v Grant (1828) 4 Bing 653

Revocation of offer

Best CJ:

'Here is a proposal [or offer] by the defendant to take property on certain terms; namely, that he should be let into possession in July. In that proposal he gives the plaintiff six weeks to consider; but if six weeks are given on one side to accept an offer, the other has six weeks to put an end to it. One party cannot be bound without the other. This was expressly decided in *Cooke* v *Oxley* (1790) 3 Term Rep 653 ... As the defendant repudiated the contract ... before the expiration of the six weeks, he had a right to say that the plaintiff should not enforce it afterwards.'

Rowland v Divall [1923] 2 KB 500 Court of Appeal (Bankes, Scrutton and Atkin LJJ)

No right to sell goods - recovery of price paid

Facts

In May 1922 the plaintiff dealer bought a car from the defendant. He sold it in July, but in September the police took possession of the vehicle on the ground that it was a stolen car and that the person who had sold it to the defendant had no title to sell it. The plaintiff sued to recover the price which he had paid the defendant for the car.

Held

He was entitled to succeed as the defendant had been in breach of the condition implied by statute that he had the right to sell the car.

Bankes LJ:

'In my opinion, that cannot possible be said here. The plaintiff received nothing, no portion of what he had agreed to buy. It is quite true that a car was handed over to him, but the person who handed it over to him had no right to hand it over to him and no title to it. In these circumstances the use by the plaintiff to the extent to which he had used it seems to me to be quite immaterial in considering whether anything was done which entitles the defendant to say that the condition has been waived or converted into a warranty. In these circumstances I think that the right of the plaintiff to recover the whole of the purchase money remains, and that the view taken by the learned judge that he should sue in damages was not justified.'

Scrutton LJ:

'It certainly seems to me that in a case of rescission for the breach of a condition that the seller has a right to sell the goods, it cannot be that the purchaser is deprived of his right to get back the purchase money because he cannot restore the goods which, from the nature of the transaction, are not the goods of the seller at all, and which the seller has, therefore, no right to in any circumstances. For these reasons it seems to me, with deference to the learned judge below, that he came to a wrong conclusion and that the plaintiff is entitled to recover the whole of the purchase money, as and for the total failure of the consideration, inasmuch as the seller did not give that which he contracted to give, namely, the legal ownership of the car and the legal right to possession of it.'

Ryan v Mutual Tontine Westminster Chambers Association [1893] 1 Ch 116 (Court of Appeal)

Specific performance - supervision required

Facts

The defendant landlords covenanted to maintain in constant attendance a resident porter for the benefit of the plaintiff and the other tenants in the block. They appointed one Benton to this post, but he spent much of his time working as a chef, leaving his wife, charwomen and others to discharge his portering responsibilities. The plaintiff sought, inter alia, specific performance of this covenant.

Held

His claim would fail as the contract would require supervision of an order that the court was not prepared to undertake.

Saunders v Anglia Building Society [1970] 3 WLR 1078 House of Lords (Viscount Dilhorne, Lords Reid, Hodson, Wilberforce and Pearson)

Mistake - plea of non est factum

Facts

The plaintiff, executrix of Mrs Gallie, a widow aged 84, ran a boarding house in Essex with the assistance of her nephew. Her nephew had possession of the deeds of the house and she was quite content that he should use them to raise money if he so wished, so long as she could stay in the house for the rest of her life. Lee, a friend of the nephew, was a man heavily in debt. Lee had a document of sale drawn up in respect of the house and took it to Mrs Gallie for her to sign. The nephew acted as witness. When she asked what the document was, she was told by Lee that it was a deed of gift in favour of the nephew. Lee paid Mrs Gallie nothing, but raised a loan for himself on the strength of the document. When he defaulted on one of the mortgages, the building society sought to recover possession and the plaintiff raised the defence of non est factum.

Held

The building society would succeed.

Lord Reid:

'The existing law seems to me to be in a state of some confusion. I do not think that it is possible to reconcile all the decisions, let alone all the reasons given for them. In view of some general observations made in the Court of Appeal I think that it is desirable to try to extract from the authorities the principles on which most of them are based. When we are trying to do that my experience has been that there are dangers in there being only one speech in this House. Then statements in it have often tended to be treated as definitions; some latitude should be left for future developments. The true ratio of a decision generally appears more clearly from a comparison of two or more statements in different words which are intended to supplement each other.

The plea of non est factum obviously applies when the person sought to be held liable did not in fact sign the document. But at least since the sixteenth century it has also been held to apply in certain cases so as to enable a person who in fact signed a document to say that it is not his deed. Obviously any such extension must be kept within narrow limits if it is not to shake the confidence of those who habitually and rightly rely on signatures when there is no obvious reason to doubt their validity. Originally this extension appears to have been made in favour of those who were unable to read owing to blindness or illiteracy and who therefore had to trust someone to tell them what they were signing. I think that it must also apply in favour of those who are permanently or temporarily unable through no fault of their own to have without explanation any real understanding of the purport of a particular document, whether that be from defective education, illness or innate incapacity.

But that does not excuse them from taking such precautions as they reasonably can. The matter generally arises where an innocent third party has relied on a signed document in ignorance of the circumstances in which it was signed, and where he will suffer loss if the maker of the document is allowed to have it declared a nullity. So there must be a heavy burden of proof on the person who seeks to invoke this remedy. He must prove all the circumstances necessary to justify its being granted to him, and that necessarily involves his proving that he took all reasonable precautions in the circumstances. I do not say that the remedy can never be available to a man of full capacity. But that could only be in very exceptional circumstances.'

Shanklin Pier Ltd v Detel Products Ltd [1951] 2 KB 854 High Court (McNair J)

Warranty - third party caused to enter into contract

Facts

The defendants were manufacturers of paint and they assured the plaintiffs that their paint was suitable for piers and would last seven years. In consequence, the plaintiffs stipulated in their contract with a firm of painters that the defendants' paint be used. It proved unsatisfactory and lasted only three months.

Held

The defendants were liable on a collateral warranty.

McNair J:

'... I am satisfied that, if a direct contract of purchase and sale of the (paint) had then been made between the plaintiffs and the defendants, the correct conclusion on the facts would have been that the defendants gave to the plaintiffs the warranties substantially in the form alleged in the statement of claim ...'

Stilk v Myrick (1809) 2 Camp 317 King's Bench (Lord Ellenborough)

Consideration - existing obligation

Facts

In the course of a sea voyage, two seamen deserted and the captain promised the remainder of the crew extra wages if they would work the ship back to London short-handed. The crew brought an action for the extra wages.

Held

The agreement was void for want of consideration.

Lord Ellenborough:

'Before they sailed from London they had undertaken to do all that they could under all the emergencies of the voyage ... the desertion of a part of the crew is to be considered an emergency of the voyage as much as their death ... those who remain are bound by the terms of their original contract to exert themselves to the utmost to bring the ship in safely to her destined port.'

Taylor v Caldwell (1863) 3 B & S 826 Court of Queen's Bench (Blackburn J)

Frustration - destruction of hall

Facts

C agreed to hire to T a hall for the purpose of holding a concert therein. Before the day of the concert, the hall was destroyed in a fire. T cancelled the concert and C claimed the letting fee.

Held

The contract of hire was frustrated and T was not liable to pay the rent.

Thomas v Thomas (1842) 11 LJ QB 104 Queen's Bench (Lord Denman CJ, Patteson and Coleridge JJ)

Consideration - sufficiency

Facts

A man having expressed - orally - the desire that his widow should have the use of a certain house, his executors agreed that she should have such use on payment of £1 a year towards the ground-rent and her undertaking to keep the house in good and tenantable repair. The executors contended that there was no consideration for their agreement.

Held

This was not the case.

Coleridge J:

'... we are not tied to look for the legal consideration for an instrument in any particular portion of it. It is usually found at the commencement; but if we find it in any other part we are bound to use it ... Here, in another part, we find an express agreement by the person to whom the premises are to be conveyed, to pay £1 a year for a particular purpose, namely, towards the ground-rent, payable in respect of the premises, and others thereto adjoining and she enters also into a distinct agreement, that, as long as she is in possession, she will do repairs. That is a sufficient consideration ...'

Universe Tankships Inc of Monrovia v International Transport Workers' Federation
[1982] 2 WLR 803 House of Lords (Lords Diplock, Cross of Chelsea, Russell of Killowen, Scarman and Brandon of Oakbrook)

Ship 'blacked' - economic duress?

Facts

A ship was 'blacked' until union demands as to pay and conditions were satisfied. In order to have the blacking lifted, the ship owners, inter alia, made a contribution to the union's welfare fund.

Held (Lord Scarman and Lord Brandon dissenting)

This contribution was recoverable by the owners as money had and received for their use.

Lord Diplock:

'It is ... in my view crucial to the decision of the instant appeal to identify the rationale of this development of the common law. It is not that the party seeking to avoid the contract which he has entered into with another party, or to recover money that he has paid to another party in response to a demand, did not know the nature or the precise terms of the contract at the time when he entered into it or did not understand the purpose for which the payment was demanded. The rationale is that his apparent consent was induced by pressure exercised on him by that other party which the law does not regard as legitimate, with the consequence that the consent is treated in law as revocable unless approbated either expressly or by implication after the illegitimate pressure has ceased to operate on his mind. It is a rationale similar to that which underlies the availability of contracts entered into and the recovery of money exacted under colour of office, or under undue influence or in consequence of threats of physical duress.

Commercial pressure, in some degree, exists wherever one party to a commercial transaction is in a stronger bargaining position than the other party. It is not, however, in my view, necessary, nor would it be appropriate in the instant appeal, to enter into the general question of the kinds of circumstances, if any, in which commercial pressure, even though it amounts to a coercion of the will of a party in the weaker bargaining position, may be treated as legitimate and, accordingly, as not giving rise to any legal right of redress. In the instant appeal the economic duress complained of was exercised in the field of industrial relations to which very special considerations apply ...

The use of economic duress to induce another person to part with property or money is not a tort per se; the form that the duress takes may, or may not, be tortious. The remedy to which economic duress gives rise is not an action for damages but an action for restitution of property or money exacted under such duress and the avoidance of any contract that had been induced by it; but where the particular form taken by the economic duress used is itself a tort, the restitutional remedy for the money had and received by the defendant to the plaintiff's use is one which the plaintiff is entitled to pursue as an alternative remedy to an action for damages in tort.'

See also Chapter 3.

Varley v Whipp [1900] 1 QB 513 High Court (Channell and Bucknill JJ)

Sale by description - reaping machine

Facts

The plaintiffs agreed to sell a reaping machine to the defendant, stating that it was nearly new and had been used only to cut 50 or 60 acres. The defendant had not seen the machine. On delivery, he returned it to the plaintiff as not answering to description, as it was extremely old. The plaintiff sued for the price, and the defendant pleaded that there had been a breach of the condition that goods would correspond with the description implied by what is now s13 of the Sale of Goods Act 1979.

Held

The defendant's argument would prevail and he was entitled to reject the machine.

Victoria Laundry (Windsor) Ltd v Newman Industries Ltd [1949] 2 KB 528 Court of Appeal (Tucker, Asquith and Singleton LJJ)

Damages - loss of profits

Facts

The defendant engineers agreed to sell a boiler to the plaintiff launderers and dyers, knowing the nature of the plaintiffs' business, that the boiler was needed for that business and that it was wanted for immediate use; they did not know, however, that it was required to extend the business. As a result of the fault of a third party, the boiler was damaged while it was being loaded on to the plaintiff's vehicle: delivery was therefore delayed and the plaintiffs claimed damages for breach of contract.

Held

They were entitled to succeed and the damages awarded could take account of any loss of profits resulting from the enforced delay in extending their business.

Warner Brothers Pictures Inc v Nelson [1937] 1 KB 209 High Court (Branson J)

Injunction - contract of service

Facts

Bette Davis (Mrs Nelson) contracted to appear in the plaintiffs' films and the plaintiffs alleged that, in breach of her contract, she intended to appear in another company's film. The plaintiffs sought an injunction.

Held

The injunction would be granted.

Branson J:

> 'The case before me is therefore one in which it would be proper to grant an injunction unless to do so would in the circumstances be tantamount to ordering the defendant to perform her contract or remain idle or unless damages would be the more appropriate remedy.
>
> With regard to the first of these considerations, it would, of course, be impossible to grant an injunction covering all the negative covenants in the contract. That would, indeed, force the defendant to perform her contract or remain idle; but this objection is removed by the restricted form in which the injunction is sought. It is confined to forbidding the defendant, without the consent of the plaintiffs, to render any services for or in any motion picture or stage production for anyone other than the plaintiffs.
>
> It was also urged that the difference between what the defendant can earn as a film artiste and what she might expect to earn by any other form of activity is so great that she will in effect be driven to perform her contract. That is not the criterion adopted in any of the decided cases. The defendant is stated to be a person of intelligence, capacity and means, and no evidence was adduced to show that, if enjoined from doing the specified acts otherwise than for the plaintiffs, she will not be able to employ herself both usefully and remuneratively in other spheres of activity, though not as

remuneratively as in her special line. She will not be driven, although she may be tempted, to perform the contract, and the fact that she may be so tempted is no objection to the grant of an injunction. This appears from the judgment of Lord St Leonard LC in *Lumley* v *Wagner* ...

With regard to the question whether damages is not the more appropriate remedy, I have the uncontradicted evidence of the plaintiffs as to the difficulty of estimating the damages which they may suffer from the breach by the defendant of her contract. I think it is not inappropriate to refer to the fact that, in the contract between the parties ... there is a formal admission by the defendant that her services, being "of a special, unique, extraordinary and intellectual character" gives them a particular value, "the loss of which cannot be reasonably or adequately compensated in damages" and that a breach may "cost the producer great and irreparable injury and damage" and the artiste expressly agrees that the producer shall be entitled to the remedy of injunction. Of course, parties cannot contract themselves out of the law; but it assists, at all events, on the question of evidence as to the applicability of an injunction in the present case, to find the parties formally recognising that which is now before the court as a matter of evidence, that in cases of this kind injunction is a more appropriate remedy than damages.'

Williams v Roffey Bros & Nicholls (Contractors) Ltd [1990] 1 All ER 512 Court of Appeal (Purchas, Glidewell and Russell LJJ)

Extra payment - consideration

Facts

The defendants contracted to refurbish a block of flats and sub-contracted the carpentry work to the plaintiff for £20,000: it was an implied term of the sub-contract that the plaintiff would receive interim payments according to the work completed. After the plaintiff had completed some of the work, and received interim payments of £16,200, he found himself in financial difficulty, partly because his price had been too low. Aware of these things, and facing a penalty if the main contract was not completed on time, the defendants agreed to pay the plaintiffs an additional £575 per flat on completion to ensure that the plaintiff continued with the work and completed it on time.

Held

This agreement would be enforced. Although the plaintiff had not been required to undertake any work additional to his original contract, the advantages which the defendants hoped to obtain (avoidance of penalty and the need to engage another sub-contractor) were consideration for the extra payment.

Woodhouse AC Israel Cocoa Ltd SA v Nigerian Produce Marketing Co Ltd [1972] AC 741 House of Lords (Lord Hailsham of St Marylebone LC, Viscount Dilhorne, Lords Pearson, Cross of Chelsea and Salmon)

Estoppel - representation as to payment

Facts

Nigerian sellers had for many years sold cocoa to an association to which the appellants belonged. Contracts were concluded on the association's standard form contract which provided, inter alia, for the settlement of all disputes by arbitration in London. Until 1963, the cocoa price was expressed in pounds sterling, but thereafter, at the seller's request, in Nigerian pounds and Lagos was substituted for London as the place of payment. In 1966 there were fears on the part of members of the association lest sterling were to be devalued. As a result of representations by the association, the sellers agreed in July 1967 that 'for transactions concluded from the 1st September 1967, payment may be made in pounds sterling in London or in £N in Lagos and that for transactions already concluded in £N, payment may be made in pounds sterling, provided the transfer charges are borne by the buyer concerned'. The appellants informed the sellers that they wished to avail themselves of this facility. On 29 August, the sellers wrote informing the association that circumstances beyond their control meant that they were forced to withdraw the option. On 30 September, however, the sellers wrote that 'payment can be made in sterling and in Lagos'. Subject to certain conditions, the association was told it was 'at liberty to make payments in sterling not only with contracts already entered into, but also with future contracts'. On the devaluation of the pound sterling, the buyers claimed they could discharge their contracts made before the date of devaluation by paying on delivery one pound sterling for every one Nigerian pound. The sellers disputed this.

Held

The representation of 30 September could not be construed in the way the buyers contended. It amounted to no more than a representation that the sellers would accept payment in Lagos of the sterling equivalent of the price calculated in Nigerian pounds. However, even if it could be said that the meaning of the letter was ambiguous and that the buyers could reasonably have understood it to contain a representation that the money on account could be treated as expressed in sterling it could not give rise to an estoppel because, to do so, a representation must be clear and unequivocal and if a representation was not clear and unequivocal, it was irrelevant that the representee reasonably misconstrued it and acted on it.

Wroth v Tyler [1973] 2 WLR 405 High Court (Megarry J)

Contract of sale - wife's objection

Facts

The defendant entered into an agreement to sell his bungalow, with vacant possession, to the plaintiffs for £6,050. Completion was fixed for 31 October 1971. The day after the defendant entered into the agreement, his wife, who had not shown any opposition to the sale, but who was not enthusiastic about it, entered in the Land Charges Register a notice under s1 of the Matrimonial Homes Act 1967, without informing the defendant. The entry was revealed by a notice sent by the Land Registry to the defendant's building society, which notified the defendant's solicitors who, in turn, informed the defendant. The defendant tried to persuade his wife to remove the notice, but was unsuccessful. Consequently he was unable to complete, but he offered to pay damages. The plaintiffs issued a writ in early 1972, seeking specific performance and damages in lieu or in addition. Judgment was given in December 1972.

Held

The plaintiffs were not entitled to an order for specific performance, with vacant possession or subject to the rights of occupation of the defendant's wife. However, they were entitled to damages for loss of bargain and here they would not be simply nominal. In the event, they were quantified as at the date of the judgment and they were assessed at £5,500.

Megarry J:

> 'The rule of common law is, that where a party sustains a loss by reason of a breach of contract, he is, so far as money can do it, to be placed in the same situation, with respect to damages, as if the contract had been performed.
>
> ... on principle, I would say that damages 'in substitution' for specific performance, must be a substitute, giving as nearly as may be what specific performance would have given ... the court has jurisdiction to award such damages as will put the plaintiff into as good a position as if the contract had been performed, even if to do so means awarding damages assessed by reference to a period subsequent to the date of the breach. This seems to me to be consonant with the nature of specific performance, which is a continuing remedy ... The conclusion that I have reached therefore, is that as matters stand, I ought to award damages to the plaintiffs of the order of £5,000 in substitution for decreeing specific performance ... This is a dismal prospect for the defendant but ... it is the plaintiffs who are wholly blameless.'

5 LAW RELATING TO EMPLOYMENT

Clayton (Herbert) and Jack Waller Ltd v Oliver [1930] AC 209 House of Lords (Viscount Dunedin, Lords Buckmaster, Blanesburgh, Warrington and Tomlin)

Breach of contract - measure of damages

Facts

By a contract contained in two letters, the appellants agreed to engage the respondent to play one of the three leading parts in a music play for six weeks, with an option to the appellant to re-engage the respondent for the run of the play. He was cast in one of the parts and, on reading it, he complained that it was not one of the three leading comedy parts, but the appellants refused to re-cast him and alleged that the part was a good performance of the contract. Thereupon the respondent declined to appear in the production and issued a writ against the appellants. He alleged that in addition to his salary, it was intended that he should benefit fully from the publicity given to the play and his reputation would have been enhanced by his taking a leading and consequently widely advertised part in an important West End production and that by reason of the breach of contract, he had lost the said publicity and been deprived of the advantages and reputation which would have followed a successful performance. It was found at first instance that the part given to the respondent was a trivial one.

Held

The respondent was entitled to succeed.

Lord Buckmaster:

'... No other part was offered and the result is that the appellants broke their contract. The next question is what was the measure of damages? ... the old and well established rule applied ... the damages are those that may reasonably be supposed to have been in the contemplation of the parties at the time when the contract was made as the probable result of its breach and if any special circumstances were unknown to one of the parties, the damages associated with the flowing from such breach cannot be included. Here both parties knew that as flowing from the contract, the plaintiff would be billed and advertised as appearing at the Hippodrome and in the theatrical profession this is a valuable right.

In assessing the damages, therefore, it was competent for the jury to consider that the plaintiff was entitled to compensation because he did not appear at the Hippodrome ... and in assessing those damages, they may consider the loss he suffered (1) because the Hippodrome is an important place of public entertainment and (2) that in the ordinary course he would have been "billed" and otherwise advertised as appearing at the Hippodrome. The learned judge put the matter as a loss of reputation, which I do not think is the exact expression, but he explained that as the equivalent of loss of publicity and that summarises what I have stated as my view of the true situation.'

Cook v Square D Ltd (1991) The Times 23 October Court of Appeal (Mustill, Mann and Farquharson LJJ)

Employer's duty to provide safe system of work - delegable?

Facts

The plaintiff was sent by the defendants, his employers, to work as a computer consultant in Saudi Arabia. While working there he slipped into a small hole in the tiled floor of the control room and suffered injury. The plaintiff argued that the duty to provide a safe system of work was non-delegable, that the defendants were in breach of it and that the facts were analagous to those in *McDermid* v *Nash Dredging and Reclamation Co Ltd* [1987] AC 906 where the plaintiff's claim had succeeded.

Held

The Court of Appeal rejected the analogy and held that there was no breach of duty by the defendants: the site was some 8,000 miles away and both the site occupiers and the general contractors were reliable companies who were aware of their responsibility for the safety of workers on site. The Court of Appeal did not, however, rule out the possibility that circumstances might require employers in the UK to take steps to satisfy themselves as to the safety of foreign sites, for example where a number of their employees were going to work on a foreign site or where one or two employees were going to work there for a considerable period of time.

Hivac Ltd v Park Royal Scientific Instruments Ltd [1946] Ch 169 Court of Appeal (Lord Green MR, Morton and Bucknill LJJ)

Master and servant - skilled worker - employment in spare time by a trade rival of employer

Facts

The plaintiff company employed the employees RD and GD on highly skilled work in which RD, at least, had access to highly confidential information. In their spare time the two worked secretly for a company which was in direct competition with the plaintiffs and persuaded others of the plaintiff company's employees to work for the defendant company in their spare time.

There was no evidence that these employees had divulged confidential information.

Held

The extent of the duty of fidelity owed to an employer by an employee may vary according to the nature of the employment, but, while the court would be reluctant to impose on workers restrictions which would hamper them in increasing their earnings in their spare time, in the present case the employees had knowingly, deliberately and secretly set themselves to do in their spare time something which would inflict great harm on their employers' business; and that the plaintiff company were entitled to an interlocutory injunction to restrain the employment by the defendant company of the plaintiff company's employees.

Morton LJ:

> 'It is clear that the five employees in question have not broken any express term of their contract of employment. It was not provided in their contract, for instance, that they should give their time exclusively to the work of the plaintiff company. What implied term, if any, has been broken? I am content, as Maugham LJ was content in *Wessex Dairies, Ld v Smith*, to quote from A L Smith LJ in *Robb v Green*, when he said: "I think that it is a necessary 'implication which must be engrafted on such a contract' - that is a contract of service - 'that the servant undertakes to serve his master with good faith and fidelity'."
>
> In all the circumstances of the case, have these five employees observed the obligations of good faith and fidelity? The work done for the defendants was done in what is usually described as the employees' spare time. No cases were cited to us in which work so done was held to be a breach of the obligation of fidelity to the employer. I do not propose to express any view of such a general nature as that all work done for a firm in the same line of business as the employers in the spare time of the employees is a breach of contract, but I do say that in my view the obligation of fidelity subsists so long as the contract of service subsists, and even in his spare time an employee does owe that obligation of fidelity. In my view, a prima facie case of a breach of that obligation is made out in the present case ...'

Hudson v Ridge Manufacturing Co Ltd [1957] 2 WLR 948 High Court (Streatfield J)

Employers' liability - competent staff

Facts

Over the years, Chadwick had indulged in horseplay at the expense of his fellow employees. The defendant employers were aware of this and had frequently issued reprimands and warnings. On the occasion in question Chadwick's prank caused the plaintiff a fractured wrist.

Held

The employers were liable as they had been in breach of their duty at common law to provide competent staff.

Streatfield J:

'It is really unarguable that here is a case where there did exist, as it were in the system of work, a source of danger, through the conduct of one of the employers' workmen, of which the employers knew: repeated conduct which went on over a long space of time, and which they did nothing whatever to remove, except to reprimand and go on reprimanding to no effect whatever ...

It was the duty of the employers to put a stop to such conduct. By that time they must have known that one day there might be injury if Mr Chadwick went on with this sort of conduct. He had done it before, he went on doing it and still he was allowed to remain in their employment and was not removed from it. In my judgment, therefore, the injury was sustained as a result of the employers' failure to take proper steps to put an end to that conduct, to see that it would not happen again and, if it did happen again, to remove the source of it. It was for that reason that this injury resulted. In those circumstances, although it is an unusual type of case, I have come to the conclusion that counsel for the plaintiff is right in his contention and that the employers are liable for the plaintiff's injuries.'

Lawton v BOC Transhield Ltd [1987] 2 All ER 608 High Court (Tudor Evans J)

Negligence - employer's character reference

Facts

After being employed by the defendants for ten years, the plaintiff was made redundant. He obtained temporary work and its being made permanent was dependent on character references. A reference provided by the defendants was unfavourable and the plaintiff lost his new job. He claimed damages on the ground that the defendants had negligently provided an inaccurate and/or unfair reference.

Held

His action would fail as there was ample evidence to support the defendants' opinions.

Tudor Evans J:

'So the questions are whether there was a sufficient proximity between the plaintiff and the defendants in this case, and, if so, whether there are considerations which should negative, reduce or limit the duty. In my view, there clearly was, on the facts as I have found them, a sufficient proximity or neighbourhood. The defendants knew precisely what they were being asked to do and in relation to whom and clearly foresaw the consequences of a failure to do it with care ... I hold that the defendants owed him a duty of care. But the question now arises whether they were in breach of the duty.

Although there must be some allowance for individual choice in the expression of opinion, the discharge of duty does require the exercise of reasonable care to make sure that the opinions are based on accurate facts. Another way of expressing the discharge of the duty is to ask whether a reasonably prudent employer would, on the facts as I find them to have been, have expressed the opinions which the defendants stated in the reference ... In my view ... the .... reference was honest, accurate and not negligently written.'

Paris v Stepney Borough Council [1951] AC 367 House of Lords (Lords Simonds, Normand, Oaksey, Morton of Henryton and MacDermott)

Negligence - employers' liability

Facts

The plaintiff, who had lost the sight in one eye, was employed by the defendants who knew of his condition. One day, when he was repairing a vehicle, he hit a bolt with a hammer to release it. The impact caused a piece of metal to fly off and enter his other eye, causing total loss of sight. He alleged his employers had been negligent in failing to supply him with protective goggles.

Held (Lord Simonds and Lord Morton of Henryton dissenting)

The plaintiff's claim succeeded. In assessing what a reasonable employer would do to ensure the safety of his employees, it is necessary to take into account not only the likelihood of the accident occurring, but also the gravity of its consequences. The employer's duty is owed to each individual workman and account must be taken of the relative gravity as regards each.

Lord Oaksey:

'In the present case the question is whether an ordinarily prudent employer would supply goggles to a one-eyed workman whose job was to knock bolts out of a chassis with a steel hammer while the chassis was elevated on a ramp so that the workman's eye was close to and under the bolt. In my opinion, Lynskey J was entitled to hold that an ordinarily prudent employer would take that precaution. The question was not whether the precaution ought to have been taken with ordinary two-eyed workmen.'

Price v Civil Service Commission [1978] IRLR 3 Industrial Tribunal

Sex discrimination - indirect discrimination - remedies

Facts

In replying to an advertisement for recruits into the Executive Officer grade of the Civil Service, Mrs Price discovered that candidates had to be at least seventeen and a half and not more than twenty-eight years of age.

She claimed that this qualification was an indirect discrimination against women, since far fewer women than men could comply with the age limit, because they were having or bringing up children and therefore 'out of the market'.

In 1976, the local tribunal [1976] IRLR 405 held that this age requirement did not contravene the Sex Discrimination Act.

Held

On remission: the respondents had failed to show the requirement that direct entrants to the Executive Officer grade of the Civil Service had to be under age 28 was justifiable irrespective of the sex of the person to whom it was applied as required by s1(1)(b)(ii) of the Sex Discrimination Act. The application of the upper age limit thus amounted to unlawful indirect discrimination against the applicant.

Applying the test of 'justifiable' set out by the EAT in *Steel* v *The Post Office* - that the requirement or condition must be necessary, not merely convenient, and that consideration should be given to whether there is some other non-discriminatory way of achieving the object - it could not be said that a rigid age bar of this kind was 'necessary'.

A recommendation was made that both parties use their best endeavours to agree a new upper age limit, to be decided for year of entry 1980.

Protective Plastics v Hawkins (1964) 49 DLR 2d 496 County Court of Ontario (Weaver J)

Master and servant - employee using employer's files while negotiating for employment with competitor

Facts

For a period of four months before his resignation from the plaintiff company, the defendant was actively engaged in making arrangements to leave the firm and go to work for a competitor.

During the period in question, he made use of the plaintiffs' files to collect information which he intended to use in his new job; made use of his employers' facilities to notify customers that he was leaving; generally did unsatisfactory work for the plaintiff.

During the whole of this time the defendant claimed his usual salary and, moreover, did not make known to his employer the fact that he was leaving.

Held

An employee owes a duty to his employer, quite apart from any contract, to be honest and faithful in his dealings with his employer. He should not use special information which he obtains during his employment for purposes of his own, contrary to the interests of his employer.

Accordingly, the plaintiff firm was entitled not only to recover the salary paid to the defendant for his final four months, but also to recover damages for the employee's breach of the duty of fidelity.

Weaver J:

'Upon the law, it seems quite clear to me that an employee of a company owes an obligation to his employers quite apart from any terms of the written contract, and there was no written contract in this case; the employee owes a duty to be faithful and honest in his dealings for the company, and a person, particularly occupying the position of the defendant, must, does owe a duty not to use the special information which he obtains while he is in its employ for his own purposes, contrary to the interests of the company.

Rashid v ILEA [1977] ICR 157 Employment Appeal Tribunal (Kilner-Brown J, Messrs JGC Milligan and W Sirs)

Employment - redundancy - continuous occupation

Facts

From June 1965 to July 1975, the plaintiff was engaged as a supply teacher by ILEA. He was appointed a term at a time; his pay was calculated on a daily basis, and he was not paid during the school holidays. Among the documents given to him on his initial employment was a statement that his employment terminated automatically at the end of the Christmas, Easter and Summer terms.

On being told in 1975 that there was no work for him, the employee claimed, inter alia, a redundancy payment under the Redundancy Payments Act 1965. The industrial tribunal held that he had not been employed for a long enough period to qualify for redundancy payment (or for compensation for unfair dismissal).

Held

On appeal by the employee, it was held, dismissing the appeal, that, although the employee had been employed as a supply teacher over a period of ten years, there were breaks in the period of employment between each school term; that those periods of school holidays could not be an absence from work on account of a 'temporary cessation of work' as contemplated by paragraph 5(1)(b) of Schedule 1 to the Contracts of Employment Act 1972 and, therefore, the employee had never been employed for a sufficient period of time to qualify for a redundancy payment or compensation for unfair dismissal.

Sinclair v Neighbour [1967] 2 WLR 1 Court of Appeal, Civil Division (Sellers, Davies and Sachs LJJ)

Master and servant - wrongful dismissal - acts inconsistent with continuance of confidence of master and servant

Facts

The manager of a betting shop openly, but without his employer's knowledge or consent, took £15 from the till, put in an IOU, and used the money to put a bet of his own with another betting shop.

The next day he repaid the £15. He had done this, with varying amounts, on other occasions. When the employer discovered what had happened he dismissed the manager on the spot, without notice.

At first instance the trial judge found that the manager had not acted dishonestly and therefore the manager was not entitled to dismiss him. On appeal by the employer:

Held

The manager's conduct, even if it was not dishonest, was inconsistent with his duty towards his employer and with the continuance of the confidential relationship of the master and servant between them; accordingly the employer had been entitled to dismiss the manager summarily on account of it.

Appeal allowed.

Sellers LJ:

> 'To take money out of the till in such circumstances is on the face it it incompatible and inconsistent with his (the employee's) duty. Some people might well say that to take money out of the till, when the employee knew that if he had asked if he could do it for the purpose which he might have had to disclose it would have been refused, is dishonest conduct. The question for this court to decide is whether, in the circumstances of this case, it was conduct which in its nature justified the employer instantly dismissing the employee. I think that it was. Counsel referred to some of the cases. I do not think that I need refer to them further. The whole question is whether that conduct was of such a type that it was inconsistent, in a grave way - incompatible - with the employment in which he had been engaged as a manager.
>
> There was an aggravating feature in that there were in the office two others, including one boy who was only some eighteen or nineteen years of age who had said something about borrowing money out of the till, and it was said that it had been done before. On a new manager coming in, I should have thought that the one thing that was incumbent on him was to keep the till inviolate. The practice of taking money out of the till in that way, as we all know in criminal courts, can lead to endless trouble.
>
> On the short facts of this case, and applying the law as I understand it, I would not hesitate to say that the dismissal was justified. I would allow the appeal accordingly.'

Thorn v Meggitt Engineering [1976] IRLR 241 Industrial Tribunal

Unfair dismissal - redundancy - discrimination

Facts

The applicant, a shop steward, was one of two brass capstan operators. In 1975 the respondents sold that part of their business employing the brass capstan operators. The applicant was told she would have to be made redundant. She was offered the job of another capstan operator who had a poor attendance record, but refused, saying she would not see another worker being made redundant to give her a job. She was therefore dismissed in 1975, November 27.

In January 1976 a vacancy occurred for a skilled drill and vaquablast operator. The applicant, among others, applied. She was told that at her age (53) it was much too heavy a job; and that as 'a big-busted woman' she would be unable to do the work.

Mrs Thorn claimed (i) she had been unfairly dismissed and (ii) she had been discriminated against by the company's refusal to re-engage her.

Held

The applicant's dismissal was on grounds of redundancy in that there was a diminished requirement for employees to do work as a capstan operator turning brass following the company's sale of their gas bracket business.

Even if the company had dismissed the applicant to save money in order to pay equal pay to other women as contended by the applicant, the dismissal would still be on grounds of redundancy since it does not matter what the motive was which produced the diminished requirement for employees to do work of a particular kind. If an employer reorganises his business to save money by reducing the number of his employees, the employees made surplus by the reorganisation are redundant, even though the amount of work remains the same or increases.

The applicant's dismissal on grounds of redundancy was fair. The company had agreed that the applicant be offered another post as a capstan operator but the applicant had refused it because it would have meant dismissing another employee. The applicant was wrong to reject this offer.

In refusing to engage the applicant to fill a subsequent vacancy as a radial drill operator, the respondents had not unlawfully discriminated against her on grounds of sex. Although s7(2)(a) of the Sex Discrimination Act renders it permissible to discriminate where being a man is a genuine occupational qualification for a job where the essential nature of the job calls for a man for reasons of physiology, s7(2)(a) specifically excludes physical strength or stamina from the definition. However, the company had shown that its requirement of strength and a height of over 5'8" for the operator of the drill was a justifiable requirement irrespective of the sex of the person to whom it was applied within the meaning of s1(1)(b)(ii) of the Act. Such a machine is potentially dangerous when operated by a short person, or a person of inadequate strength. Such a person could injure themselves, and the company might be liable.

Even had the applicant been discriminated against at the interview by virtue of being told that the job was much too heavy for her, that if she had been age 16 she might have been considered but that as she was a big-busted woman she could not do the job, there was no discrimination by the respondents in failing to offer the applicant the vacancy. The respondents had subsequently decided to reorganise their workforce so that there was no need to recruit from outside and no outside applicant for the vacancy was successful. Hence Mrs Thorn was not treated less favourably than any male applicant.

Woodhouse v Brotherhood [1972] 3 WLR 215 Court of Appeal, Civil Division (Lord Denning MR, Buckley and Raskill LJJ)

Master and servant - continuity of employment - redundancy

Facts

C Ltd, an engineering firm, owned a factory in Derbyshire where they manufactured diesel engines.

In 1965 they sold the factory and adjoining land to PB Ltd who made spinning machines, compressors and steam turbines.

PB agreed to complete for C at C's cost four or five diesel engines, then in the process of being built. After the sale C Ltd carried on business at their factory in Manchester, as the sale to PB did not include a transfer of goodwill.

All but one of the employees continued to work at the Derbyshire factory, on the same terms and conditions. There was no break in their employment. Although there was a change in the finished product the employees used the same tools and equipment for PB as they had for C. The applicants had worked for 34 and 18 years respectively for C and for six years for PB when they were made redundant by PB. They claimed that their earlier service for C should be taken into account in working out length of service.

PB appealed against the National Industrial Relations Court's decision that the applicants had been continuously employed.

Held

To determine whether there had been a transfer of a business for the purposes of para 10(2) of the Contracts of Employment Act 1965 it was necessary to look at the nature of the business and to ask whether, by the sale, the purchaser had become the proprietor of the business in succession to the vendor; the test of whether the transaction had affected the working environment of the employees was not the right test to apply. All that PB Ltd had acquired on the sale were the physical assets, ie the buildings, plant and equipment; they had not acquired C Ltd's trade or business, which had been transferred to Manchester; the business which PB Ltd carried on at the factory was a different business from that which had been carried on by C Ltd; the production unit acquired by PB Ltd was not used to carry on any trade or business acquired from C Ltd. Accordingly since the sale did not constitute a transfer of a business within para 10(2) of Sch 1 to the 1963 Act, and the applicants had been employed in a different business from the date of the sale in 1965, their period of employment with C Ltd did not count in assessing their entitlement to redundancy payments from PB Ltd. They were therefore entitled to redundancy payments only in respect of the six years of employment with PB Ltd and the appeal would be allowed.

6 FAMILY LAW

Cossey v UK [1991] 2 FLR 492; [1991] Fam Law 362 European Court of Human Rights

Where parties are not respectively male and female

Facts

The applicant was born a male but subsequently underwent a sex change operation and thereafter lived as a woman. She complained to the European Court of Human Rights that she had been refused a birth certificate stating that she was female, and that all public documents, such as her passport, stated her gender as male. In addition, she complained that she could not legally marry a man under the law of the United Kingdom. This interference in her life was alleged to violate both Articles 8 and 12 of the European Convention on Human Rights.

Held

Articles 8 (right to family life) and 12 (right to marry) of the European Convention on Human Rights were not violated (following *Rees* v *UK* [1987] 2 FLR 111). It was held that article 12 referred to the traditional marriage between persons of the opposite biological sex. The UK law's attachment to the traditional concept of marriage was sufficient reason for the continued adoption of biological criteria to determine a person's sex for the purpose of marriage. With reference to article 8, the refusal to issue a birth certificate was not an interference with the right to respect private life. A fair balance had to be struck between the general interest of the community and the interests of the individual. The register of births was a public system to accurately record evidence of facts at birth, to establish family connections (eg to determine legitimate descent), and for statistical study of population and growth. Following *Rees* v *UK* that system was not unfair to Miss Cossey. However, the court was conscious of the serious problems facing transsexuals and the law would be kept under review in light of current circumstances.

Ffinch v Combe [1894] P 191 Probate Division

Will - obliteration of words - meaning of the term 'apparent'

Facts

Slips of paper, which could have been removed leaving the document intact, were, after the execution of a will, pasted over certain words in it. These words could be read by an expert in writing on placing a piece of brown paper over them and holding the document to a window.

By s21 of the Wills Act then current:

> 'No obliteration interlineation or other alteration made in any will after the execution thereof shall be valid or have any effect, except so far as the words or effect of the will before such alteration shall not be apparent, unless such alteration shall be executed in like manner as hereinbefore is required for the execution of the will.'

> Words beneath obliterations, erasures, or alterations on a testamentary document are "apparent" within the meaning of the section, if experts using magnifying glasses, when necessary, can decipher them and satisfy the Court that they have done so; but it is not allowable to resort to any physical interference with the document, so as to render clearer what may have been written upon it.'

Probate was originally granted, omitting words on the strips of paper as it was assumed they had been incorporated after the execution of the will.

It was sought to have probate granted as including certain words on strips of paper.

Held

Such concealment amounted to 'obliteration' of the words; but, as the original could be read by a graphology expert, they would be considered 'apparent' within the Act.

The original version of the will would stand and the strips of paper be discounted.

The President of the Probate Division:

'The difficulty in the present and in several cases which have been decided is, What is the meaning of the word "apparent" within this section? No case exactly like the present appears hitherto to have arisen. But there are several cases which, dealing with erasures and alterations made of or over words in a testamentary document, shew in what cases words so obscured are considered to be "apparent", and by what means they may be made so "apparent".

The first of these cases is that of *In the Goods of Sir Charles Ibbetson* (1), decided in 1839. In that case Sir Herbert Henner Fust said: "The obliterations and erasures should be carefully examined by persons accustomed to inspect writings, in order to ascertain how the will originally stood. Possibly with the use of glasses that may be discovered; but I am quite unable to make it out." In that case, as it turned out, it could not be discovered what the parts obscured originally were.

In the case of *In the Goods of Beavan* (2), decided by the same learned judge in the following year, a word had been altered, but in such a way that the original word remained, beyond question, apparent. In that case probate was granted with the original word.

A more important case is that of *Townley* v *Watson* (3), decided in 1844. In that case the question dealt with by the same learned judge was whether the words in question must be themselves apparent, or whether they might be proved by extrinsic evidence. The learned judge said, referring to the 21st section of the Wills Act: "What, then, is the interpretation to be put on this section, when either words in a will or the effect of words are so completely effaced or obliterated as not to be apparent? Now, I think the prima facie construction must be '*apparent on the face of the instrument itself*', and not that suggested in argument - namely, 'capable *of being made apparent*' by extrinsic evidence. What is an obliteration? Is it not by some means covering over words originally written so as to render them no longer legible? I cannot understand, if the legislature really intended that extrinsic evidence should be admitted, why a few more words were not added which would have freed the section from all doubt; for instance, why was it not thus penned, 'Unless the words should be capable of being made apparent.' There may be inconsistencies, and there may be inconveniences - I do not say there are - in the construction I am putting on the section; but I think it impossible to read the words and not say, it was the intention of the legislature, that if a testator shall take such pains to obliterate certain passages in his will, and shall so effectually accomplish his purpose that those passages cannot be made out on the face of the instrument itself, it shall be a revocation as good and valid as if done according to the stricter forms mentioned in the Act of Parliament.'

(1)   2 Curt 337   (2)   2 Curt 369   (3)   3 Curt 761

Hyde v Hyde (1866) 12 LT 235

Family law

Facts

Case concerned marriage and its status. Best known for the decision and in particular pronouncement of Lord Penzance.

Held

Marriage is the voluntary union for life of one man and one woman to the exclusion of all others.

Ibbetson, In the Goods of (1839) 2 Curt 337

See reference in *Ffinch* v *Combe* above.

Jones, Re [1981] 2 WLR 106 Family Division (Sir John Arnold, President)

Law relating to soldiers' wills

Facts

Jones was serving in the army in Northern Ireland. He had already made a formal will, leaving all his property to his mother.

In 1978 he was shot and said while dying, in the presence of two army officers 'See Anne gets all my stuff, if I do not make it.'

He died the next day.

Held

The verbal statement constituted a valid informal will (a soldier's will). The earlier will, leaving his property to his mother was therefore replaced by that in favour of Anne, his fiancée.

Stokes v Anderson [1991] 1 FLR 391; [1991] Fam Law 310 Court of Appeal (Lloyd, Nourse and Ralph Gibson LJJ)

Resulting trust - cohabitation - contributions to house expenses

Facts

Mr Stokes and Miss Anderson lived together but were not married. Mr Stokes had been married before. He and his ex-wife owned the former matrimonial home in equal shares. He had bought his ex-wife's share for £45,000. Miss Anderson gave him £5,000 and then £7,000 towards the £45,000. They planned to get married but Mr Stokes cancelled the plans. Miss Anderson then lived in the house. She decorated it and worked in the garden spending £2,500 of her own money. The relationship broke down. Mr Stokes applied for possession saying that the payments made by Miss Anderson had been loans and gave rise to no interest in the house. Miss Stokes claimed a beneficial interest. She was awarded a half share in the house. Mr Stokes appealed.

Held

The evidence was that there was a common intention that Miss Anderson should have a beneficial interest. She paid the money on the understanding that they would marry and that the house would be their home. Her payments of sums totalling £12,000 constituted conduct amounting to an acting on the common intention by her. The extent of her beneficial interest had never been discussed by the parties. Its quantification depended upon the parties' common intention, not necessarily ascertained at the time the interest was acquired, but seen in the light of all payments made and the acts done by Miss Anderson so as to arrive at the determination of a fair share. A fair result, bearing in mind that Mr Stokes had already a half share in the house and only needed to acquire his ex-wife's half share at the time of Miss Anderson's first payment, was that Miss Anderson was entitled to one half of that half share, ie one quarter of the whole, subject to the mortgage (*Gissing* v *Gissing* [1971] AC 886 and *Grant* v *Edwards* [1986] Ch 638 followed).